IGCSE
Mathematics

University of Cambridge Local Examinations Syndicate

Reviewed by **John Pitts**, Principal Examiner and
Moderator for HIGCSE Mathematics

Edited by **Carin Abramovitz**

CAMBRIDGE
UNIVERSITY PRESS

PUBLISHED BY THE PRESS SYNDICATE OF THE UNIVERSITY OF CAMBRIDGE
The Pitt Building, Trumpington Street, Cambridge CB2 1RP, United Kingdom

CAMBRIDGE UNIVERSITY PRESS
The Edinburgh Building, Cambridge CB2 2RU, UK http://www.cup.cam.ac.uk
40 West 20th Street, New York, NY 10011-4211, USA http://www.cup.org
10 Stamford Road, Oakleigh, Melbourne 3166, Australia
Dock House, Victoria and Alfred Waterfront, Cape Town 8001, South Africa

First published 1997
Fourth printing 2002

Printed by Creda Communications, Cape Town

Typeface New Century Schoolbook 11.5/14 pt

A catalogue record for this book is available from the British Library

ISBN 0 521 62518 1 paperback

Acknowledgements
We would like to acknowledge the contribution made to these materials by the writers and
editors of the Namibian College of Open Learning (NAMCOL).

Illustrations by André Plant.

Contents

Introduction

Welcome to Module 2 of IGCSE Mathematics! This is the second **module** in a course of six modules designed to help you prepare for the International General Certificate of Secondary Education (IGCSE) Mathematics examinations. Before starting this module, you should have completed Module 1. If you are studying through a distance-education college, you should also have completed the **end-of-module assignment** for Module 1. The diagram below shows how this module fits into the IGCSE Mathematics course as a whole.

Module 1	Module 2	Module 3	Module 4	Module 5	Module 6
Assignment 1	Assignment 2	Assignment 3	Assignment 4	Assignment 5	Assignment 6

Like the previous module, this module should help you develop your mathematical knowledge and skills in particular areas. If you need help while you are studying this module, contact a **tutor** at your college or school. If you need more information on writing the examination, planning your studies, or how to use the different features of the modules, refer back to the **Introduction** at the beginning of Module 1.

Some study tips for Maths

- As you work through the course, it is very important that you use a **pen or pencil and exercise book**, and *work through* the examples yourself in your exercise book as you go along. Maths is not about reading, but about doing and understanding!
- Do feel free to write in pencil in this book – fill in steps that are left out and make your own notes in the margin.
- *Don't expect to understand everything the first time you read it.* If you come across something difficult, it may help if you read on – but make sure you come back later and go over it again until you understand it.
- You will need a **calculator** for doing mathematical calculations and a **dictionary** may be useful for looking up unfamiliar words.

Remember

- In the examination you will be required to give decimal approximations correct to **three significant figures** (unless otherwise indicated), e.g. 14.2 or 1 420 000 or 0.00142.
- Angles should be given to **one decimal place**, e.g. 43.5°. Try to get into the habit of answering in this way when you do the exercises.

The **table** below may be useful for you to keep track of where you are in your studies. Tick each block as you complete the work. Try to fit in study time whenever you can – if you have half an hour free in the evening, spend that time studying. Every half hour counts! You can study a **section**, and then have a break before going on to the next section. If you find your concentration slipping, have a break and start again when your mind is fresh. Try to plan regular times in your week for study, and try to find a quiet place with a desk and a good light to work by. Good luck with this module!

IGCSE MATHEMATICS MODULE 2

Unit no.	Unit title	Unit studied	'Check your progress' completed	Revised for exam
1	Algebraic Representation and Formulae			
2	Indices			
3	Algebraic Manipulation			
4	Solving Equations and Inequalities			

Unit 1
Algebraic Representation and Formulae

In everyday life and in our work we often see symbols which we have to interpret. How many of the following can you interpret?

USA H_2SO_4 IGCSE   R10   K2P2Sℓ1K1psso πr^2

You probably had no trouble with USA (United States of America), IGCSE (International General Certificate of Secondary Education) and R10 (10 Rands). Do you know that 'rand' is a shortened form of 'Witwatersrand'? If you have studied chemistry, you will know that H_2SO_4 is the formula for sulphuric acid.

K2P2Sℓ1K1psso will only make sense to you if you know something about knitting. It comes from a knitting pattern and tells you to knit 2 (stitches), purl 2, slip 1, knit 1 and pass the slipped stitch over.

πr^2 is used in mathematics and it should be familiar to you. It is the formula for calculating the area of a circle which has a radius of length r.

Each of the symbols above is part of a language which you learn in order to understand a subject. πr^2 is an example of algebraic language which you will be studying in this module.

This unit has four sections:

Section	Title	Time
A	The language of algebra	2 hours
B	Solving linear equations	1 hour
C	Changing the subject of a formula	1 hour
D	Constructing equations and formulae	2 hours

By the end of this unit, you should be able to:

- use letters to represent generalised numbers or unknown numbers
- express basic arithmetical processes algebraically
- substitute numbers for words and letters in formulae
- simplify algebraic expressions
- solve simple linear equations
- transform simple formulae
- construct algebraic equations from given situations
- deal with direct and inverse proportion algebraically.

A The language of algebra

In algebra, letters are used to represent numbers. Sometimes a letter may stand for lots of numbers (as in a formula). In other cases a letter will stand for a particular number whose value is unknown to begin with – the problem is to work out its value (as in an equation).

Examples

1. The area of a rectangle is
    length × breadth.
    This can be written in algebra as
    $A = L \times B$.
    Here L units is the length of
           the rectangle,
           B units is the breadth
    and A square units is the area.
    A, L and B can stand for lots of numbers.

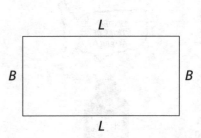

2. The statement $n + 2 = 8 - n$ tells you that if 2 is added to the number n, the result is the same as taking the number n away from 8. This is only true for one particular number. n has to be 3. Statements such as $n + 2 = 8 - n$ are called **equations** and finding the particular number which makes an equation true is called **solving the equation**. I'll show you how to solve equations later in this unit.

3. 3×7 gives the same answer as 7×3. This is just one example of a property of multiplication of numbers. (It is called the commutative property of multiplication.)
    Here are some more examples:

    $15 \times 9 = 9 \times 15, \quad 3.14 \times 23.5 = 23.5 \times 3.14, \quad \frac{3}{4} \times \frac{5}{9} = \frac{5}{9} \times \frac{3}{4}.$

    In algebraic language, this property of multiplication is written as 'If a and b are numbers, then $a \times b = b \times a$'.

Try these questions:

EXERCISE 1

> The *perimeter* of a rectangle is the total length of all the sides.

1. To find the perimeter of a rectangle, you double the length and add on double the breadth.
    Write this formula in algebraic language.

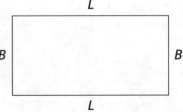

2. Look at these statements:
    $2 + 5 = 5 + 2, \quad 4.7 + 10.5 = 10.5 + 4.7, \quad \frac{3}{4} + \frac{1}{8} = \frac{1}{8} + \frac{3}{4}.$
    These are just three of many examples we could have used to illustrate the commutative property of addition of numbers. Using a and b to represent the two numbers, write down a statement in algebraic language which is true for all numbers.

3. Write down in words what the following algebraic statement tells you about the number n:
    $5n - 8 = n + 20$

4. a) Using n to represent the number, write the following
        statement in algebraic language:
            If you multiply the number by 3 and take away 7,
            you get 5 more than the number.
    b) n can only be one particular number. What is it?

5. Using k to represent the number, write the following statement
    in algebraic language:
            If you multiply the number by itself and take away 3,
            you get double the number.

Check your answers at the end of this module.

Symbols and algebraic shorthand

Vuyile and Shireen were both asked to work out $5t^2$ when t is 2.

Vuyile did it this way   Shireen did it this way

| t is 2 |
| so $5t$ is 10 |
| so $5t^2$ is 10^2 |
| $= 100$ |

| $5t^2 = 5 \times t^2$ |
| $= 5 \times 2^2$ |
| $= 5 \times 4$ |
| $= 20$ |

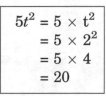 

Who was right?

To answer this you must understand the rules of algebra. $5t^2$ means
that t is squared (that means t is multiplied by itself) and the result
is multiplied by 5. Shireen understood this and so she had the right
answer. Vuyile multiplied t by 5 and then squared the result.
In algebraic language this would be written as $(5t)^2$.

Here is a list of some statements in algebra. Make sure you
understand the meaning of all of them.

Statement	Meaning
$a = b$	a is equal to b
$a \neq b$	a is not equal to b
$a < b$	a is less than b
$a \leqslant b$	a is less than or equal to b
$a > b$	a is greater than b
$a \geqslant b$	a is greater than or equal to b
$a + b$	b is added to a
$a - b$	b is subtracted from a
$a \times b$ or ab	a is multiplied by b
$a \div b$ or a/b or $\frac{a}{b}$	a is divided by b
a^2	the square of a. That is, $a \times a$
a^5	a to the power of 5. That is, $a \times a \times a \times a \times a$
$a - (b + c)$	b and c are added and the result is subtracted from a
ab^2	a is multiplied by the square of b. That is, $a \times b \times b$
$(ab)^2$	a is multiplied by b and the result is squared. That is, $(a \times b) \times (a \times b)$ which is equal to a^2b^2

Examples

1. When $a = 2$ and $b = 3$,
    the value of the expression ab^2 is $2 \times 3^2 = 2 \times 9 = 18$
    and the value of the expression $(ab)^2$ is $(2 \times 3)^2 = 6^2 = 36$.

2. When $x = 7$, $y = 8$ and $z = 5$,
    the value of the expression $x - (y - z)$ is $7 - (8 - 5) = 7 - 3 = 4$
    and the value of the expression $x - y - z$ is $7 - 8 - 5 = -1 - 5 = -6$.

3. Suppose you are y years old and your mother is m years old.
    'Your mother is more than twice as old as you' would be written
    as $m > 2y$. 'You are 25 years younger than your mother' would
    be written as $y = m - 25$.

4. I think of a number, which we will represent by n. 'I double the
    number and take away 7' in algebraic shorthand is $2n - 7$.
    'My answer is 35' gives us the equation $2n - 7 = 35$.

5. The area of a triangle can be obtained by multiplying the base
    by the height and dividing the result by 2.
    In algebraic shorthand this is

    $$A = \frac{bh}{2}$$

    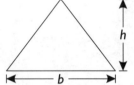

    where b units is the length of the base
               h units is the height
    and A square units is the area

6. Suppose you are y years old and your father is f years old.
    The algebraic statement $y + f = 50$ would tell you that your age
    and your father's age add up to 50 years. The algebraic
    statement $f > y + 20$ would tell you that your father is more
    than 20 years older than you.

Now test your understanding of algebraic language by doing the
following exercise.

EXERCISE 2

1. Given $p = 6$ and $q = 2$, find the value of:
    a) $p^2 - q^2$ b) $(p - q)^2$

2. Given that $x = 5$, $y = 2$ and $z = 3$, find the value of:
    a) $x - (y + z)$ b) $x - y + z$

3. Suppose you are y years old and your brother is b years old.
    Write in algebraic shorthand:
    a) your brother is older than you
    b) your brother is twice as old as you

4. I think of a number, square it, double the answer and then take
    away 15. My answer is 377. Using n to represent the number I
    thought of, write down an equation in algebraic language.

5. To find the area of an ellipse, you multiply the major diameter by the minor diameter, then multiply the result by π and divide by 4. Write this formula in algebraic shorthand.

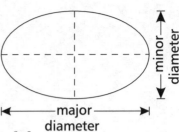

Check your answers at the end of this module.

Using formulae

Formulae are used in mathematics, science, surveying and in many other subjects. They may be written in words or in algebraic language.

For example, in words,
the perimeter of a rectangle is twice the length plus twice the breadth.
In algebraic language, it is $P = 2L + 2B$.

'Using a formula' involves replacing letters (or words) with particular numbers. This process is called **substitution**.

If you understand algebraic language, you should have no trouble with substitution.

Examples

1. The formula for the perimeter of a rectangle is $P = 2L + 2B$.
    When $L = 8$ and $B = 3$, $P = 2 \times 8 + 2 \times 3 = 16 + 6 = 22$.

2. A car is travelling along a road with a speed of v kilometres per hour. The driver has to make an emergency stop because a pedestrian steps on to the road.

    The distance the car travels before it stops is d metres. The formula for d is $d = \dfrac{v(v + 32)}{150}$.

    If the car is travelling at 48 km per hour,
    $$d = \frac{48(48 + 32)}{150} = \frac{48 \times 80}{150} = \frac{3840}{150} = 25.6$$
    The stopping distance is 25.6 m.

3. The area of a rhombus is the product of the diagonals divided by 2. If the diagonals are 9 cm and 5 cm long, the area of the rhombus is
    $$9 \times 5 \div 2 = 45 \div 2 = 22\tfrac{1}{2} \text{ cm}^2.$$

    'Product of diagonals' means that one diagonal is multiplied by the other.

4. The cost, C Rands, of printing n books is given by the formula
    $$C = 12n + 750.$$
    When $n = 300$, $C = 12 \times 300 + 750 = 3600 + 750 = 4350$.
    This means that the cost of printing 300 books is R4350.

5. $I = \dfrac{E}{R + r}$ is a formula used by electricians.
    When $E = 28$, $R = 3$, and $r = 2$, $I = \dfrac{28}{3 + 2} = \dfrac{28}{5} = 5.6$.

    The capital letter R and the small letter r are treated as different – they stand for different things.

Try these now:

EXERCISE 3

1. Use the formula $P = 2L + 2B$ to find the value of P:
   a)   when $L = 12$ and $B = 7$
   b)   when $L = 4.6$ and $B = 3.5$

2. A car is travelling at 100 km per hour. Use the formula
   $d = \dfrac{v(v + 32)}{150}$ to find its stopping distance in metres.

3. Use the formula $C = 12n + 750$ to find the value of C:
   a)   when $n = 5$
   b)   when $n = 500$

4. From a point h metres above the surface
   of the sea, the distance to the horizon
   is d kilometres. The formula for d is
   $d = 3.55 \sqrt{h}.$
   The top of a lighthouse is
   32 m above the surface
   of the sea.
   Use the formula to calculate
   the distance to the horizon
   from the top of the
   lighthouse.

5. The volume of a pyramid is
   the area of its base times its perpendicular
   height divided by 3.
   Calculate the volume of a pyramid
   which has a square base with side 5 cm
   and a perpendicular height of 6 cm.

Check your answers at the end of this module.

Simplifying algebraic expressions

Suppose you were asked to work out the value of the expression $2a + 3a + 5a$ for various values of a.

For example,   when $a = 8$, $2a + 3a + 5a = 16 + 24 + 40 = 80$
                  and when $a = 12$, $2a + 3a + 5a = 24 + 36 + 60 = 120$.

It would not take you long to realise that the value of the expression is always 10 times the value of a.

We can write $2a + 3a + 5a = 10a$ for all values of a and we say that this is simplifying the expression by 'adding like terms'.

You cannot simplify the expression $2a + 3b + 5c$ until you know the values of a, b and c because $2a$, $3b$ and $5c$ are not like terms.

You should also recognise that $a^2 + 4a + 5$ cannot be simplified because a^2, $4a$ and 5 are not like terms.

Here are some examples of expressions which can be simplified (at least to some extent):

$4a + 6b + 3a = 7a + 6b$ $\boxed{4a + 3a = 7a}$

$5x + 2y - x = 4x + 2y$ $\boxed{5x - x = 4x}$

$2p + 5q + 3q - 7p = -5p + 8q$ $\boxed{2p - 7p = -5p \text{ and } 5q + 3q = 8q}$

$\boxed{-5p + 8q \text{ could be written as } 8q - 5p}$

$x^2 - 3x + 4 + 2x^2 - 5x - 7 = 3x^2 - 8x - 3$

$8c - 2c + 5d - 6c + 4d = 9d$ $\boxed{8c - 2c - 6c = 0}$

$2x + 3xy - 5 + 6yx = 2x - 5 + 9xy$ $\boxed{yx = xy \text{ so } 3xy \text{ and } 6yx \text{ are like terms}}$

Here are some examples of expressions which cannot be simplified because they contain no like terms:

$2xy - x - y - 2$

$a^3 + a^2 - 3a + 4$

$p^2q + pq^2 + 5pq$

Some expressions contain brackets and these usually have to be removed before the expression can be simplified.

To remove the brackets in $2(3a + 5b)$ you have to remember that, just as $2x = x + x$, so $2(3a + 5b) = (3a + 5b) + (3a + 5b)$

so $2(3a + 5b) = 6a + 10b$

Similarly,

$2(4x - y) = (4x - y) + (4x - y) = 8x - 2y$

$3(3c - 2d) = (3c - 2d) + (3c - 2d) + (3c - 2d) = 9c - 6d$

$4(p + 2q) = (p + 2q) + (p + 2q) + (p + 2q) + (p + 2q) = 4p + 8q$

A *term* is separated from another *term* by a '+' or '−' sign.

Can you see that a quicker way of getting the answers above would be to multiply every term inside the brackets by the number outside the brackets.

So $\quad 8(2a - 3b) = 16a - 24b$

$12(x^2 + 3x - 2) = 12x^2 + 36x - 24$

$5(cd + c - 3d) = 5cd + 5c - 15d$

Now see how to simplify an expression such as $2(3x + y) + 5(x - 2y)$ by removing the brackets:

$2(3x + y) + 5(x - 2y)$ $\boxed{\text{remove brackets}}$

$= 6x + 2y + 5x - 10y$ $\boxed{\text{add like terms}}$

$= 11x - 8y$

Here are a few more examples which you should find easy to follow:

$4(2n + 3) + 7(n + 1) = 8n + 12 + 7n + 7 = 15n + 19$

$3(x - 2) + 2(3 - x) = 3x - 6 + 6 - 2x = x$

$6(3x^2 + 2x) + 3x - 5 = 18x^2 + 12x + 3x - 5 = 18x^2 + 15x - 5$

Now it's time for you to test your understanding of the work we have just done by tackling the questions in Exercise 4.

EXERCISE 4

1. Find the value of $2n + 7n - 3n$:
   a) when $n = 8$
   b) when $n = 72$

2. Simplify the following expressions where possible.
   a) $3p + 7q - 2p - 5q$
   b) $4n - 4 + 3n + 1$
   c) $2x^3 + 3x^2 - x^2 + 5x$
   d) $3xy - 3 + y$
   e) $2c - 5d + d - 3c$
   f) $x^2 + 4x - 3 - 7x + 9$

3. Remove the brackets in the following expressions.
   a) $4(4x - 3)$
   b) $7(2n + 5)$
   c) $8(6 - 2y)$
   d) $3(2x^2 + 3x - 5)$
   e) $6(5pq - p - 2q)$

4. Remove the brackets and collect like terms to simplify the following.
   a) $3(n + 5) + 4(2n - 3)$
   b) $7(2x - 1) + 2(3 - x)$
   c) $5y - 3 + 3(4y - 2)$
   d) $2(6c + 5d) + 6(d - 2c)$
   e) $8(x^2 + x - 3) + 5(2 - x)$

Check your answers at the end of this module.

B Solving linear equations

Suppose I said to you 'I start with a number, double it and add 5. My answer is 33'. Could you work out the number I started with?

Perhaps you would use trial and error, trying various numbers until you found the right one.

Or perhaps you would use a logical arithmetical method such as:
If my answer was 33, I must have had 28 before 5 was added.
That means that I must have had 14 before the number was doubled.
So the number I started with must have been 14.

Simple problems like this can usually be solved by arithmetical methods. But it is useful to see how they can be solved by algebra because algebraic methods are much more useful in solving more complicated problems.

If we use n to represent the number I started with, the statement I made can be written as $2n + 5 = 33$.

This is an equation and you have to find the value of n which makes the left-hand side equal to the right-hand side. This is sometimes written as 'find the value of n which satisfies the equation' or 'solve the equation'.

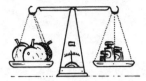

To solve an equation, we must keep the two sides equal or 'balanced'. The two sides will remain balanced if you:

- add the same number to both sides
- subtract the same number from both sides
- multiply both sides by the same number
- divide both sides by the same number.

What you want to do when you solve equations like

$$an + b = cn + d \qquad \text{(where } a, b, c, d \text{ are numbers)}$$

is to use the above facts and finish with $n = \ldots$

Equations of this form are called **linear equations**. The reason for this will become clear when you study algebraic graphs in Module 3.

Starting with $\qquad\qquad 2n + 5 = 33$

you subtract 5 from both sides   [this undoes the 'add 5' in the equation]

$$2n + 5 - 5 = 33 - 5$$
$$\text{so } 2n = 28$$

now you divide both sides by 2   [this undoes the 'multiply by 2']

So the answer is $n = 14$.

Here are some more equations to solve. Make sure you have a pencil and paper so that you can try them yourself. Don't just read the examples.

Example 1

Solve the equation $3x - 8 = 39$.

Solution

(Here the 'unknown number' is x not n.)

$$3x - 8 = 39$$
$$3x - 8 + 8 = 39 + 8 \qquad \text{[add 8 to both sides]}$$
$$\text{that is } 3x = 47 \qquad \text{[divide both sides by 3]}$$
$$\text{so } x = 15\tfrac{2}{3}$$

Example 2

Solve the equation $n + 2 = 8 - n$.

Solution

$$n + 2 = 8 - n \qquad \text{[subtract 2 from both sides]}$$
$$n = 6 - n \qquad \text{[add } n \text{ to both sides – you don't want } n \text{ on the right-hand side]}$$

$$n + n = 6 - n + n$$
$$\text{that is } 2n = 6 \qquad \text{[divide both sides by 2]}$$
$$\text{so } n = 3$$

Example 3

Solve the equation $3n - 7 = n + 5$.

Solution

$$3n - 7 = n + 5 \quad \boxed{\text{add 7 to both sides}}$$
$$3n = n + 12 \quad \boxed{\text{subtract } n \text{ from both sides}}$$
$$2n = 12 \quad \boxed{\text{divide both sides by 2}}$$
$$\text{so } n = 6$$

Example 4

Solve the equation $2(y - 4) = 18$.

Solution

Method A:

$$2(y - 4) = 18 \quad \boxed{\text{divide both sides by 2}}$$
$$(y - 4) = 9 \quad \boxed{\text{add 4 to both sides}}$$
$$\text{so } y = 13$$

Method B:

$$2(y - 4) = 18 \quad \boxed{\text{remove brackets}}$$
$$2y - 8 = 18 \quad \boxed{\text{add 8 to both sides}}$$
$$2y = 26 \quad \boxed{\text{divide both sides by 2}}$$
$$\text{so } y = 13$$

Example 5

Solve the equation $3(n - 4) + 2(4n - 5) = 5(n + 2) + 16$.

Solution

To solve this more complicated equation we must first simplify both sides by removing the brackets and collecting like terms.

$$3n - 12 + 8n - 10 = 5n + 10 + 16 \quad \boxed{\text{remove brackets and add like terms}}$$
$$11n - 22 = 5n + 26 \quad \boxed{\text{add 22 to both sides}}$$
$$11n = 5n + 48 \quad \boxed{\text{subtract 5}n \text{ from both sides}}$$
$$6n = 48 \quad \boxed{\text{divide both sides by 6}}$$
$$n = 8$$

As you get more practice solving equations you will see that you won't need to write every step. Look at this example again from the step $11n - 22 = 5n + 26$. I know that I want all the terms with n on the left-hand side and all the terms without n on the right-hand side.

So I can write this as the next step:

$$11n - 5n = 26 + 22 \quad \boxed{\text{make sure you understand how I did this}}$$
$$\text{so } 6n = 48$$
$$\text{and } n = 8$$

Example 6

A rough rule for changing temperatures in degrees Celsius (C) to degrees Fahrenheit (F) is $F = 2C + 30$.
a)   Find the value of F when $C = 25$.
b)   Find the value of C when $F = 20$.

Solution

a) $C = 25$
     so $F = 2 \times 25 + 30 = 50 + 30 = 80$
b) $F = 20$
     so $20 = 2C + 30$

This is an equation which we have to solve.

$20 - 30 = 2C$ $\boxed{\text{subtract 30 from both sides}}$
so $-10 = 2C$ $\boxed{\text{divide both sides by 2}}$
$-5 = C$
so $C = -5$

Now you should have some practice in solving equations. Here are some for you.

EXERCISE 5

1.   Solve the equation $5x + 3 = 38$.

2.   Solve the equation $4n - 1 = n + 8$.

3.   Solve the equation $6(x + 2) = 42$.

4.   Solve the equation $7(y - 3) + 5 = 4(2 - y) + 3y$.

5.   When I treble a certain number and add 2, I get the same answer as I do when I take the number from 50. Let n represent the number. Write an equation for n and solve it.

6.   A rough rule for changing temperatures in degrees Fahrenheit (F) to degrees Celsius (C) is $C = \frac{1}{2}F - 15$.
     a)   Find the value of C when $F = 70$.
     b)   Find the value of F when $C = 30$.

Check your answers at the end of this module.

C   Changing the subject of a formula

One of the formulae used in mechanics is $v = u + at$.

(You can take v to be the speed of a car which had a speed of u and then accelerated at a rate a for time t.)

This formula is useful for calculating the value of v when you know the values of u, a and t.

We say that v is the **subject** of the formula.

The formula is not so useful if you want to calculate the value of t when you know the values of the other letters. We would like to have a formula which is of the form

t = an expression containing v, u and a.

We say that we need to **change the subject of the formula** or that we need to **transform the formula**.

Changing the subject of a formula is equivalent to solving an equation for the required letter.

Compare these two problems and the solutions:

Given that $84 = 36 + 4t$, find the value of t.	Given that $v = u + at$, find the formula for t.
$84 = 36 + 4t$ $$84 - 36 = 4t$$ $$48 = 4t$$ $$12 = t$$ The solution is $t = 12$.	$v = u + at$ $$v - u = at$$ $$\frac{v-u}{a} = t$$ The formula is $t = \frac{v-u}{a}$.

The steps you take to change the subject of a formula are exactly the same as those you take to solve an equation. Here is a reminder. You can:

- add the same number to both sides $\boxed{\text{if } x - b = a, \text{ then } x = a + b}$
- subtract the same number from both sides $\boxed{\text{if } x + b = a, \text{ then } x = a - b}$
- multiply both sides by the same number $\boxed{\text{if } \frac{x}{b} = a, \text{ then } x = ab}$
- divide both sides by the same number. $\boxed{\text{if } bx = a, \text{ then } x = \frac{a}{b} \text{ provided } b \neq 0}$

In addition to these four steps, there are two others which are sometimes useful in transforming formulae (or solving equations). You can:

- square both sides $\boxed{\text{if } \sqrt{x} = a, \text{ then } x = a^2}$
- take the square root of both sides. $\boxed{\text{if } x^2 = b, \text{ then } x = \pm\sqrt{b}}$

> If $x = 3$ then $x^2 = (3)^2 = 9$.
> If $x = -3$ then $x^2 = (-3)^2 = 9$
> so if $x^2 = 9$ then $x = 3$ or $x = -3$
> which you can write as $x = \pm 3$.

As an example, take $A = \pi r^2$ which is the formula to find the area (A) of a circle when you know its radius (r).

How can you calculate the radius of a circle if you know its area?

You need to transform the formula so that its subject is r.

This is how you do it:

$$A = \pi r^2$$

Divide both sides by π $\frac{A}{\pi} = r^2$

Take the square root of both sides $\pm\sqrt{\frac{A}{\pi}} = r$

Now you must think. In this example r stands for the radius of a circle. You cannot have a '$-$' radius. So you only use the '$+$' answer.

So the required formula is $r = \sqrt{\frac{A}{\pi}}$.

Example 1

Change the subject of the formula of $S = 2n - 4$ to n.

Solution

$$S = 2n - 4$$
$$S + 4 = 2n$$
$$\frac{S + 4}{2} = n$$

The required formula is $n = \frac{S + 4}{2}$.

Example 2

A formula used in electricity is $C = \frac{E}{R}$.

Change the subject of the formula to R.

Solution

$$C = \frac{E}{R} \qquad \boxed{\text{multiply both sides by } R}$$
$$CR = E \qquad \boxed{\text{divide both sides by } C}$$
$$\text{so } R = \frac{E}{C}$$

Example 3

a) Solve the equation $\frac{x}{2} - 3 = 5$.

b) Change the subject of the equation $\frac{x}{a} - b = c$ to x.

Solution

a) $$\frac{x}{2} - 3 = 5$$
$$\frac{x}{2} = 8$$
$$\text{so } x = 16$$

b) $$\frac{x}{a} - b = c$$
$$\frac{x}{a} = c + b$$
$$x = a(c + b)$$

Since $c + b = b + c$, the required formula can be written as $x = a(b + c)$.

Example 4

A formula used in electricity is $E = V + IR$.

a) Find the value of R when $E = 20$, $V = 15$ and $I = 2$.

b) Express R in terms of E, V and I.

Solution

a) You have to find the value of R which satisfies the equation.
$$20 = 15 + 2R$$
$$\text{so } 5 = 2R$$
$$2.5 = R$$
So the required value of R is 2.5.

b) 'Express R in terms of E, V and I' means the same as 'Change the subject of the formula to R'.

In this part, you take exactly the same steps as in part a).

$$E = V + IR$$

so $E - V = IR$

$$\frac{E - V}{I} = R$$

The required formula is $R = \frac{E - V}{I}$.

Example 5

Change the subject of the formula $m = \frac{y - c}{x}$ to y.

Solution

$$m = \frac{y - c}{x} \quad \boxed{\text{multiply both sides by } x}$$
$$mx = y - c$$
$$mx + c = y$$

So the required formula is $y = mx + c$.

Example 6

Change the subject of the formula $f = \frac{v^2}{r}$ to v.

Solution

$$f = \frac{v^2}{r}$$
$$\text{so } fr = v^2 \quad \boxed{\text{take the square root on both sides}}$$
$$\pm\sqrt{fr} = v$$

The required formula is $v = \pm\sqrt{fr}$.

You need lots of practice now. Do the following exercise.

EXERCISE 6

1. a)   Solve the equation $47 = 3x + 8$.
    b)   Change the subject of the formula $y = 3x + 8$ to x.

2. a)   Solve the equation $4x + 5 = 17$.
    b)   Given the $ax + b = c$, express x in terms of a, b and c.

3. Change the subject of the formula $v = u + at$ to u.

4. A formula used for a pulley system is $P = \frac{1}{2}W + 6$.
    Change the subject of the formula to W.

5. If $2x + 3y = 12$, find a formula for y in terms of x.

6. Change the subject of the formula $C = 2\pi r$ to r.

7. Change the subject of the formula $S = \sqrt{1.5H}$ to H.

8. Change the subject of the formula $E = \frac{Wv^2}{2g}$ to v.

When you have tried all these questions, look at the solutions at the end of this module. Many learners find this work difficult so don't be surprised if some of your answers are wrong. I have given full solutions to help you. Use them to see where you went wrong and then do the questions again until you can do them on your own.

D Constructing equations and formulae

Solving problems

It is very unlikely that, in your everyday life at home and at work, anyone would say to you 'What is the solution of the equation $4x - 5 = 31$?'

But, you may be asked to solve a problem or a puzzle expressed in everyday language which you decide to tackle by using algebra.

The steps you should take are as follows:

- make sure you understand the problem – read it carefully
- note the facts which are given and the quantities you have to find
- state clearly the letter (usually x or n) which you will use to represent one of the quantities you have to find
- represent the other unknown quantities in terms of the letter
- write down an equation using facts which have been given
- solve the equation
- state clearly the values of the quantities you were asked to find
- check your answer – make sure it is reasonable and fits the given facts.

Example 1

In 5 years' time, Nanjula will be three times as old as she was 9 years ago. How old is she now?

Solution

Let her present age be n years. In 5 years' time she will be $(n + 5)$ years old. 9 years ago she was $(n - 9)$ years old. In 5 years' time Nanjula will be three times as old as she was 9 years ago.

So we can write the equation

$$\underbrace{(n + 5)}_{\text{in 5 years}} = \underbrace{3(n - 9)}_{\text{9 years ago}}$$

$$\text{so } n + 5 = 3n - 27$$
$$n + 32 = 3n$$
$$32 = 2n$$
$$16 = n$$

So Nanjula's present age is 16 years.
(Check: In 5 years' time she will be 21 years old,
    9 years ago she was 7 years old,
and this fits the facts because $21 = 3 \times 7$.)

Example 2

Vuyokazi gives a quarter of her sweets to Nodumo and then gives 5 of her sweets to Phumlani. She has 7 sweets left. How many sweets did she have at the beginning?

Solution

Let n be the number of sweets Vuyokazi had at the beginning. After giving a quarter of them to Nodumo, she had $\frac{3}{4}n$ left. After giving 5 to Phumlani, she had $\frac{3}{4}n - 5$ left. We are told that Vuyokazi had 7 sweets left so we can write the equation

$$\frac{3}{4}n - 5 = 7$$

$$\frac{3}{4}n = 12 \quad \boxed{\text{multiply both sides by 4}}$$

$$3n = 48$$

$$n = 16$$

At the beginning Vuyokazi had 16 sweets.
(Check: After giving Nodumo 4 sweets, Vuyokazi had 12 left and after giving Phumlani 5 sweets, she had 7 left.)

Example 3

The distance round a rectangular field is 400 m, The length of the field is 26 m more than the breadth. Calculate the length and breadth of the field.

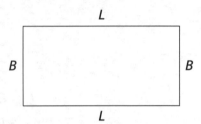

Solution

Let the breadth of the field be x metres. Then the length is $(x + 26)$ metres. The distance round the field is 400 m so we can write the equation

$$x + (x + 26) + x + (x + 26) = 400$$

$$\text{so} \qquad 4x + 52 = 400$$

$$4x = 348$$

$$x = 87$$

> Always read the question again to make sure you have answered it.

The breadth of the field is 87 m and the length is 113 m.
(Check: Distance round the field = 87 + 113 + 87 + 113 = 400 m.)

Example 4

A rubber costs 15 cents more than a pencil. 12 pencils cost 60 cents more than 8 rubbers. Find the cost of one pencil.

Solution

Let the cost of one pencil be p cents. Then the cost of one rubber is $(p + 15)$ cents. 12 pencils cost 60 cents more than 8 rubbers so we can write the equation

$$12p = 8(p + 15) + 60$$

$$\text{so } 12p = 8p + 120 + 60$$

$$12p = 8p + 180$$

$$4p = 180$$

$$p = 45$$

One pencil costs 45 cents.
(Check: 12 pencils cost 540 cents and 8 rubbers cost 8×60 cents = 480 cents.)

Upstream means *against* the current.
Downstream means *with* the current

Example 5

A river cruiser travelled upstream for 7 hours and then returned downstream to its starting point in 3 hours. The cruiser's speed in still water is 15 km/h. Find the speed of the river current.

Solution

Let the speed of the river current be x kilometres per hour. Travelling upstream (against the current), the cruiser's speed is $(15 - x)$ km/h and in 7 hours it travels $7(15 - x)$ km.   (distance = speed × time)
Travelling downstream (with the current), the cruiser's speed is $(15 + x)$ km/h and in 3 hours it travels $3(15 + x)$ km.
The distance travelled upstream is the same as the distance travelled downstream, so we can write the equation

$$7(15 - x) = 3(15 + x)$$
$$\text{so } 105 - 7x = 45 + 3x$$
$$105 = 45 + 10x$$
$$60 = 10x$$
$$6 = x$$

The speed of the river current is 6 km/h.
(Check: Upstream the cruiser travels at 9 km/h and travels 63 km in 7 hours and downstream it travels at 21 km/h and travels 63 km/h in 3 hours.)

Now try some problems on your own. Remember to follow the steps I gave at the beginning of this section. Good luck!

EXERCISE 7

1. In 7 years' time, Jan will be twice as old as he was 8 years ago. How old is he now?

2. Temba is twice as old as Sipho and Silo is 5 years younger than Sipho. The total of their ages is 31 years. How old is Sipho?

3. Marcus bought a pizza and cut it into three pieces. When he weighed the pieces, he found that one piece was 7 g lighter than the largest piece and 4 g heavier than the smallest piece. The whole pizza weighed 300 g. How much did each of the three pieces weigh?

4. Herman rowed upstream a certain distance and then rowed downstream back to his starting point. Altogether the journey took 2 hours. In still water, Herman rows at 8 km/h but the stream was flowing at 2 km/h. How many kilometres did Herman row upstream?

5. Last season, Dickson attended all 21 home matches of his favourite football team. Sometimes he bought a ticket for a seat costing R45. On the other occasions he bought a ticket to stand and this cost R25. For the whole season Dickson paid R765 for his tickets. How many times did he buy a ticket for a seat?

Check your answers at the end of this module.

Finding a formula for a sequence

Remember that we looked at sequences in Module 1? What is the next number in the sequence 1, 4, 9, 16, 25, ... ? It's 36.

How did I know? I can see a pattern:

number of term	1	2	3	4	5
pattern	$(1)^2$	$(2)^2$	$(3)^2$	$(4)^2$	$(5)^2$
term	1	4	9	16	25

fill in this row first

when I try to find a pattern I want the number of the term to be part of the pattern

fill in this row second

I can also see that term 16 will be $(16)^2$, in fact the **general term** or **n^{th} term** will be n^2.

What is the nth term of the sequence $\frac{1}{2}$, $\frac{2}{3}$, $\frac{3}{4}$, $\frac{4}{5}$, $\frac{5}{6}$, ... ?
Let's find the pattern:

number of term	1	2	3	4	5
pattern	$\frac{1}{1+1}$	$\frac{2}{2+1}$	$\frac{3}{3+1}$	$\frac{4}{4+1}$	$\frac{5}{5+1}$
term	$\frac{1}{2}$	$\frac{2}{3}$	$\frac{3}{4}$	$\frac{4}{5}$	$\frac{5}{6}$

Can you see that the nth term will be $\frac{n}{n+1}$?

Try this one: 2, 4, 6, 8, 10, ...

number of term	1	2	3	4	5
pattern	2(1)	2(2)	2(3)	2(4)	2(5)
term	2	4	6	8	10

The nth term is $2n$.

What about the nth term for this sequence: 5, 8, 11, 14, 17, ... It's a little more tricky to find the pattern here. I'm going to show you a way of finding the formula for the nth term of a sequence like this where the numbers increase or decrease by the same amount each time.

In the sequence 5, 8, 11, 14, 17, ... the numbers increase by 3 each time. So the formula will contain $3n$. Now find the pattern:

number of term	1	2	3	4	5
pattern	3(1) + 2	3(2) + 2	3(3) + 2	3(4) + 2	3(5) + 2
term	5	8	11	14	17

So the nth term in this case is $3n + 2$.

Here's another one: 3, 7, 11, 15, 19, ... Each term increases by 4. So I know there will be a $4n$ in the formula. Look at the first term, which is 3. For the first term, $n = 1$. $4n = 4(1) = 4$. Subtract 1 and I get 3.

Let me try term 2. $4n = 4(2) = 8$. Subtract 1 and I get 7. Check a few more to make sure that the formula for a term of this sequence is $4n - 1$.

Work through the following examples. Try to work them out yourself before you read my solution.

Example 1

Find the formula for the nth term of the sequence 1, 3, 5, 7, 9, ...

Solution

The numbers increase by 2 each time so the formula contains $2n$. $2n$ alone would give the sequence 2, 4, 6, 8, 10, ... Each number must be decreased by 1 to match the given sequence. The nth term of 1, 3, 5, 7, 9, ... is therefore $2n - 1$.

Example 2

Find the formula for the nth term of the sequence 20, 17, 14, 11, 8, ...

Solution

The numbers *decrease* by 3 each time so the formula contains $-3n$. $-3n$ alone would give the sequence $-3, -6, -9, -12, -15, \ldots$ Each number must be increased by 23 to match the given sequence. The nth term of 20, 17, 14, 11, 8, ... is therefore $-3n + 23$ (or $23 - 3n$).

Example 3

Find the formula for the nth term of the sequence $-8, -3, 2, 7, 12, \ldots$

Solution

The numbers increase by 5 each time so the formula contains $5n$. $5n$ alone would give the sequence 5, 10, 15, 20, 25, ... Each number must be decreased by 13 to match the given sequence. The nth term of $-8, -3, 2, 7, 12, \ldots$ is therefore $5n - 13$.

Example 4

Find the formula for the nth term of the sequence $3, 3\frac{1}{2}, 4, 4\frac{1}{2}, 5, \ldots$

Solution

The numbers increase by $\frac{1}{2}$ each time so the formula contains $\frac{1}{2}n$. $\frac{1}{2}n$ alone would give the sequence $\frac{1}{2}, 1, 1\frac{1}{2}, 2, 2\frac{1}{2}, \ldots$ Each number must be increased by $2\frac{1}{2}$ to match the given sequence. The nth term of $3, 3\frac{1}{2}, 4, 4\frac{1}{2}, 5, \ldots$ is therefore $\frac{1}{2}n + 2\frac{1}{2}$.

EXERCISE 8

1. Find the formula for the nth term of the sequence $5, 7, 9, 11, 13, \ldots$

2. Find the formula for the nth term of the sequence $2, 5, 8, 11, 14, \ldots$

3. Find the formula for the nth term of the sequence $12, 10, 8, 6, 4, \ldots$

4. Find the formula for the nth term of the sequence $1\frac{1}{2}, 2, 2\frac{1}{2}, 3, 3\frac{1}{2}, \ldots$

5. Write down the formula for the nth term of $1, 8, 27, 64, 125, \ldots$

Check your answers at the end of this module.

Direct and inverse proportion

You will remember that in Module 1 we studied proportion from an arithmetical point of view. We will now look at more complicated cases of proportion using algebraic methods.

Direct proportion

If the values of two variables P and Q are always in the same ratio, the variables are said to be in direct proportion. We write $P \propto Q$ for 'P is **directly proportional** to Q'.

$P \propto Q$ means $\frac{P}{Q}$ = constant. That is $P = kQ$, where k is a constant.

So, for example, $P = 2Q$ means that whatever Q is P will always be double that value.

So $\frac{P}{Q} = 2$.

Inverse proportion

If the product of the values of two variables P and Q is constant, the variables are said to be in inverse proportion. 'P is **inversely proportional** to Q' means that $PQ = k$, where k is a constant.

You will notice that $PQ = k$ could be written as $P = \frac{k}{Q}$ and so 'P is inversely proportional to Q' can be written as $P \propto \frac{1}{Q}$.

Working through some examples will help you to understand these ideas.

Example 1

y is directly proportional to x^3. When $x = 2$, $y = 32$.
Find the value of y when $x = 5$.

Solution

y is directly proportional to x^3 means that
$y = kx^3$ where k is a constant. Find out what this constant is.
When $x = 2$, $y = 32$ so $32 = 8k$.
This means that $k = 4$ and that $y = 4x^3$.
It follows that, when $x = 5$, $y = 4 \times 5^3 = 4 \times 125 = 500$.

Example 2

F is inversely proportional to d^2. When $d = 3$, $F = 12$.
Find the value of F when $d = 4$.

Solution

F is inversely proportional to d^2 means that
$$F = \frac{k}{d^2} \text{ where } k \text{ is a constant.}$$
When $d = 3$, $F = 12$ so $12 = \frac{k}{9}$ and so $k = 108$.

The formula connecting F and d is $F = \frac{108}{d^2}$.

So, when $d = 4$, the value of $F = \frac{108}{16} = 6.75$.

Example 3

q	2	5	8	12
p	2.8	7	11.2	16.8

Some corresponding values of the variables p and q are shown in the table. Are p and q directly proportional?

Solution

$\frac{2.8}{2} = 1.4$, $\frac{7}{5} = 1.4$, $\frac{11.2}{8} = 1.4$, $\frac{16.8}{12} = 1.4$

The ratios of corresponding values are all equal so p and q are directly proportional. The formula connecting them is $p = 1.4q$.

Example 4

x	3	4	5	6	7
y	12				

Complete this table:
a)   when $y \propto x$
b)   when $y \propto \frac{1}{x}$

Solution

a) $y \propto x$ means that $y = kx$ and since $y = 12$ when $x = 3$, it follows that $k = 4$. The formula connecting y and x is $y = 4x$ and the completed table is:

x	3	4	5	6	7
y	12	16	20	24	28

b) $y \propto \frac{1}{x}$ means that $y = \frac{k}{x}$ or $xy = k$. Since $y = 12$ when $x = 3$, it follows that $k = 36$. The formula connecting y and x is $y = \frac{36}{x}$ and the completed table is:

x	3	4	5	6	7
y	12	9	7.2	6	5.14

Example 5

The speed of water in a river is determined by a water-pressure guage. The speed (v m/s) is directly proportional to the square root of the height (h cm) reached by the liquid in the guage. Given that $h = 36$ when $v = 8$, calculate the value of v when $h = 18$.

Solution

$v \propto \sqrt{h}$ means that $v = k\sqrt{h}$ where k is constant.

When $v = 8$, $h = 36$ and so $8 = k\sqrt{36} = 6k$.

It follows that $k = \frac{4}{3}$ and the formula connecting v and h is $v = \frac{4}{3}\sqrt{h}$.

When $h = 18$, $v = \frac{4}{3}\sqrt{18} = \frac{4}{3} \times 4.2426 = 5.66$ to 3 significant figures.

Time now for you to try some questions on direct and inverse proportion.

EXERCISE 9

1. A is directly proportional to r^2. When $r = 3$, $A = 36$.
    Find the value of A when $r = 10$.

2. I is inversely proportional to d^3. When $d = 2$, $I = 100$.
    Find the value of I when $d = 5$.

3.

q	2	5	8	12
p	75	30	20	15

    Some corresponding values of the variables p and q are given in the table. Are p and q inversely proportional?
    Justify your answer.

4. An electric current I flows through a resistance R. I is inversely proportional to R and, when $R = 3$, $I = 5$. Find the value of I when $R = 0.25$.

5.

s	2	6	10
t	0.4	10.8	50

    Some corresponding values of the variables s and t are given in the table. Which of the following types of proportion fits these values?
    $$t \propto s, \quad t \propto s^2, \quad \text{or} \quad t \propto s^3$$

Check your answers at the end of this module.

Summary

You have now completed the work in Unit 1. In this unit you should have become familiar with the language of algebra. There are some important rules to remember:

* to simplify algebraic expressions you can add or subtract *like* terms
* to solve an equation remember that whatever you do to one side *you must do to the other side as well*

- changing the subject of the formula is similar to solving an equation – you rearrange the equation so that the required variable is on one side and all the other variables are on the other side of the '=' sign.

In the work on direct and inverse proportion you learnt that:

- $P \propto Q$ means P is directly proportional to Q. That is $P = kQ$.
- $P \propto \frac{1}{Q}$ means P is inversely proportional to Q. That is $PQ = k$.

In the next unit you will learn about indices.

Check your progress

1. At a party, there are c children, w women and m men. Write each of the following statements in terms of algebra, using appropriate mathematical symbols.
    a)   There are 14 people at the party.
    b)   There are more than three children.
    c)   The number of men is different from the number of children.
    d)   There are two more women than men.

2. Find the value of $\sqrt{\frac{a^2 + b^2}{6}}$ when $a = 5.3$ and $b = 4.8$.

3. $S = 13 + 5R$.
    a)   If $R = 2.8$, find the value of S.
    b)   If $S = 48$, find the value of R.
    c)   Make R the subject of the formula.

4. Solve the following equations.
    a) $4x = 34$
    b) $\frac{y}{5} = \frac{3}{4}$
    c) $5(z + 2) = 3(z - 1) + 23$

5.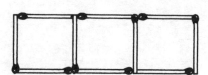

    The diagrams above show how matchsticks are used to make lines of squares.
    a)   Complete the following table.

number of squares in line	1	2	3	4	5	6	7	8
number of matchsticks needed	4	7	10					

    b)   How many matchsticks are needed to make 6 squares in a line?
    c)   Find the formula for the number of matches needed to make n squares in line.

6. A builder has to deliver 20 tonnes of sand to a customer. He has a large truck which holds 3 tonnes of sand and a small truck which holds 2 tonnes. His driver makes x journeys with the large truck and y journeys with the small truck, each time fully loaded.
   a) Write down an equation connecting x to y.
   b) State why x and y must be whole numbers.
   c) Write down all the possible pairs of values of x and y.

7. y is inversely proportional to x^2, and $y = 1.5$ when $x = 12$. Calculate the value of y when $x = 3$.

Check your answers at the end of this module.

Unit 2
Indices

Welcome to working with indices – a very useful way to work with numbers, if you know how! Knowing how to work with indices will be easy if you *understand* what indices are. So work carefully and always with a pencil and paper so that you get lots of practice.

This unit has four sections:

Section	Title	Time
A	Working with positive indices	3 hours
B	Zero and negative indices	2 hours
C	Writing numbers in standard form	3 hours
D	Fractional indices	1 hour

By the end of this unit you should be able to:

- interpret positive, negative and zero indices
- use the laws of indices
- simplify algebraic expressions involving indices
- write and use numbers in standard form
- interpret fractional indices.

A Working with positive indices

2^5 is shorthand for $2 \times 2 \times 2 \times 2 \times 2$ and you say '2 to the power 5'.
5^2 is shorthand for 5×5 and you say '5 to the power 2' or '5 squared'.
6^3 is shorthand for $6 \times 6 \times 6$ and you say '6 to the power 3' or '6 cubed'.

Indices is the plural of index.

Power is another word for index.

$6^3 = 6 \times 6 \times 6$
$6^3 \neq 6 \times 3$
When you write the power make sure it is small and at the top.

$a^1 = a$

$$a^n = a \times a \times a \ldots (n \text{ times})$$

the **index** or **power**

the **base**

Work through these examples carefully:

Example 1

Calculate the value of:
a) 6^4
b) $2^4 \times 3^4$
c) $4^3 \div 2^5$
d) $\left(\frac{2}{3}\right)^4$

Solution

a) $6^4 = 6 \times 6 \times 6 \times 6 = 36 \times 6 \times 6 = 216 \times 6 = 1296$
b) $2^4 \times 3^4 = (2 \times 2 \times 2 \times 2) \times (3 \times 3 \times 3 \times 3) = 16 \times 81 = 1296$
c) $4^3 \div 2^5 = (4 \times 4 \times 4) \div (2 \times 2 \times 2 \times 2 \times 2) = 64 \div 32 = 2$
d) $(\frac{2}{3})^4 = \frac{2}{3} \times \frac{2}{3} \times \frac{2}{3} \times \frac{2}{3} = \frac{16}{81}$

Example 2

Calculate the value of:
a) $2^2 \times 2^5$
b) 2^7
c) $3^2 \times 3^3$
d) 3^5

Solution

a) $2^2 \times 2^5 = (2 \times 2) \times (2 \times 2 \times 2 \times 2 \times 2) = 4 \times 32 = 128$
b) $2^7 = 2 \times 2 \times 2 \times 2 \times 2 \times 2 \times 2 = 128$
c) $3^2 \times 3^3 = (3 \times 3) \times (3 \times 3 \times 3) = 9 \times 27 = 243$
d) $3^5 = 3 \times 3 \times 3 \times 3 \times 3 = 243$

Example 3

Calculate the value of:
a) $2^6 \div 2^4$
b) 2^2
c) $10^5 \div 10^2$
d) 10^3

Solution

a) $2^6 \div 2^4 = (2 \times 2 \times 2 \times 2 \times 2 \times 2) \div (2 \times 2 \times 2 \times 2) = 64 \div 16 = 4$
b) $2^2 = 2 \times 2 = 4$
c) $10^5 \div 10^2 = (10 \times 10 \times 10 \times 10 \times 10) \div (10 \times 10)$
$$= 100\,000 \div 100 = 1000$$
d) $10^3 = 10 \times 10 \times 10 = 1000$

Example 4

Calculate the value of:
a) $(0.2)^3$
b) 2^6
c) $(2^3)^2$
d) $(10^4)^3$

Solution

a) $(0.2)^3 = 0.2 \times 0.2 \times 0.2 = 0.008$
b) $2^6 = 2 \times 2 \times 2 \times 2 \times 2 \times 2 = 64$
c) $(2^3)^2 = (2^3) \times (2^3) = 8 \times 8 = 64$
d) $(10^4)^3 = (10^4) \times (10^4) \times (10^4) = 10\,000 \times 10\,000 \times 10\,000 = 1\,000\,000\,000\,000$

Now do some calculations yourself.

EXERCISE 10

1. Calculate the value of:
   a) $2^3 \times 5^3$
   b) $2^8 \div 8^2$
   c) $(\frac{3}{5})^4$
   d) 1^8

2. Calculate the value of:
   a) $4^2 \times 4^3$
   b) 4^5
   c) $6^3 \times 6$
   d) 6^4

3. Calculate the value of:
   a) $3^5 \div 3^3$
   b) 3^2
   c) $10^6 \div 10^4$
   d) 10^2

4. Calculate the value of:
   a) $(1.1)^4$
   b) $(3^2)^3$
   c) $(3^3)^2$
   d) $(10^2)^4$

Check your answers at the end of this module.

The rules of indices

Instead of writing the numbers out each time you may have worked out that there are some short cuts you can take. These are the rules for working with indices. Let's look at them:

$2^3 \times 2^5$ = (three 2s multiplied together) $\times$ (five 2s multiplied together)

= eight 2s multiplied together

= 2^8

So $2^3 \times 2^5 = 2^{3+5}$

---

the first rule of indices $a^m \times a^n = a^{m+n}$

This can be written as $a^{\text{any index}} \times a^{\text{any index}} = a^{\text{sum of the indices}}$
The bases of the numbers being multiplied *must be the same*.
When numbers with the same base are being divided, there is a similar rule. For example,

$7^5 \div 7^2$ = (five 7s multiplied together) $\div$ (two 7s multiplied together)

$= \dfrac{7 \times 7 \times 7 \times 7 \times 7}{7 \times 7}$

$= 7 \times 7 \times 7$ two of the 7s in the numerator are cancelled out by the two 7s in the denominator

$= 7^3$

This shows that $7^5 \div 7^2 = 7^{5-2}$.

> the second rule of indices $a^m \div a^n = a^{m-n}$

Another way to write this is

$$a^{\text{any index}} \div a^{\text{any index}} = a^{\text{first index} - \text{second index}}$$

Again, it is important to remember that the bases of the numbers being divided *must be the same*.

The third rule of indices is concerned with expressions such as $(2^3)^4$, where there are two indices (3 and 4 in this example) on the same base (2 in this example).

You know that $(2^3)^4 = 2^3 \times 2^3 \times 2^3 \times 2^3$

$$= 2^{3+3+3+3} \quad \boxed{\text{using the first rule of indices}}$$

$$= 2^{3 \times 4}$$

$$= 2^{12}$$

In general, $(a^m)^n = a^m \times a^m \times a^m \times \ldots (n \text{ times})$

$$= a^{m+m+m+\ldots(n \text{ times})} \boxed{\text{using the first rule of indices}}$$

$$= a^{mn} \quad \boxed{\text{because there were n 'm's added in the index}}$$

> the third rule of indices $(a^m)^n = a^{mn}$

You can write this as $(a^{\text{any index}})^{\text{any index}} = a^{\text{product of the indices}}$

Learn these rules well now by doing the following examples.

Example 1

Use the first rule of indices to simplify:
a) $5^4 \times 5^2$
b) $6^{23} \times 6^{17}$
c) $7^2 \times 7^3 \times 7^4$
d) $3 \times 3^4 \times 3^5$

Solution

a) $5^4 \times 5^2 = 5^{4+2} = 5^6$
b) $6^{23} \times 6^{17} = 6^{23+17} = 6^{40}$
c) $7^2 \times 7^3 \times 7^4 = 7^{2+3+4} = 7^9$
d) $3 \times 3^4 \times 3^5 = 3^1 \times 3^4 \times 3^5 = 3^{1+4+5} = 3^{10}$

Example 2

Use the second rule of indices to simplify:
a) $7^{10} \div 7^2$
b) $9^6 \div 9^4$
c) $8^{12} \div 8^{11}$
d) $3^5 \div 3$

Solution

a) $7^{10} \div 7^2 = 7^{10-2} = 7^8$
b) $9^6 \div 9^4 = 9^{6-4} = 9^2$
c) $8^{12} \div 8^{11} = 8^{12-11} = 8^1 = 8$
d) $3^5 \div 3 = 3^5 \div 3^1 = 3^{5-1} = 3^4$

Example 3

Use the third rule of indices to simplify:
a) $(4^3)^5$
b) $(4^5)^3$
c) $(10^7)^2$
d) $[(2^3)^4]^5$

Solution

a) $(4^3)^5 = 4^{3 \times 5} = 4^{15}$
b) $(4^5)^3 = 4^{5 \times 3} = 4^{15}$
c) $(10^7)^2 = 10^{7 \times 2} = 10^{14}$
d) $[(2^3)^4]^5 = [2^{3 \times 4}]^5 = [2^{12}]^5 = 2^{12 \times 5} = 2^{60}$

Example 4

Use the rules of indices to express each of the following in the form a^n.
a) $3^4 \times 3^5 \div 3^2$
b) $4^5 \times 4^6 \div 4^{10}$
c) $[2^8 \div 2^5]^3$
d) $(5^4)^3 \times 5$

Solution

a) $3^4 \times 3^5 \div 3^2 = 3^{4+5} \div 3^2 = 3^9 \div 3^2 = 3^{9-2} = 3^7$
b) $4^5 \times 4^6 \div 4^{10} = 4^{5+6} \div 4^{10} = 4^{11} \div 4^{10} = 4^{11-10} = 4^1 = 4$
c) $[2^8 \div 2^5]^3 = [2^{8-5}]^3 = [2^3]^3 = 2^{3 \times 3} = 2^9$
d) $(5^4)^3 \times 5 = 5^{4 \times 3} \times 5 = 5^{12} \times 5 = 5^{12} \times 5^1 = 5^{12+1} = 5^{13}$

To make sure that you have grasped the three rules of indices, do the following exercise.

EXERCISE 11

1. Use the first rule of indices to simplify:
    a) $8^3 \times 8^2$
    b) $4^4 \times 4^4$
    c) $6^3 \times 6^2 \times 6^7$
    d) $5^3 \times 5^8 \times 5$

2. Use the second rule of indices to simplify:
    a) $3^8 \div 3^2$
    b) $2^{20} \div 2^5$
    c) $4^6 \div 4^5$
    d) $7^7 \div 7$

3. Use the third rule of indices to simplify:
   a) $(5^2)^4$
   b) $(5^4)^2$
   c) $(9^8)^3$
   d) $[(4^2)^3]^5$

4. Use the rules of indices to express each of the following in the form a^n.
   a) $2^6 \times 2^3 \div 2^4$
   b) $6^3 \times 6^5 \div 6^7$
   c) $(3^5 \div 3^3)^4$
   d) $(8^3)^3 \div 8^4$

Check your answers at the end of this module.

The rules of indices in algebra

So far you have worked with indices in arithmetical situations. In algebra, letters are used to represent numbers and so the rules of indices which you have learnt in arithmetic apply equally to algebra. It is important though to remember the other forms of shorthand that are used in algebra. For example,

ab means $a \times b$

and ab^3 means $a \times b^3$ (that is $a \times b \times b \times b$)

Notice that the power (or index) applies only to the base to which it is attached. In our example, the 'cube' applies only to the base b and not to the number a.

If you want the 'cube' to apply to the 'a' as well as to the 'b', you must either write the power '3' on the 'a' as well as on the 'b' or put brackets round ab. This means that you write a^3b^3 or $(ab)^3$.

Example 1

Given that $p = 2$ and $q = 5$, calculate the value of:

a) p^3q^2

b) $2p^4 + 3q^3$

c) $(3p)^2$

d) $3q^2 - 4q + 8$

Solution

a) $p^3q^2 = (p \times p \times p) \times (q \times q) = (2 \times 2 \times 2) \times (5 \times 5) = 200$

b) $2p^4 + 3q^3 = (2 \times p \times p \times p \times p) + (3 \times q \times q \times q)$
$$= (2 \times 2 \times 2 \times 2 \times 2) + (3 \times 5 \times 5 \times 5)$$
$$= 32 + 375 = 407$$

c) $(3p^2) = (3p) \times (3p) = 6 \times 6 = 36$

d) $3q^2 - 4q + 8 = (3 \times q \times q) - (4 \times q) + 8$
$$= (3 \times 5 \times 5) - (4 \times 5) + 8$$
$$= 75 - 20 + 8$$
$$= 55 + 8 = 63$$

Example 2

Use the first rule of indices to simplify:

a) $2e^4 \times 5e^{10}$

b) $5y^5 \times 3y^3$

c) $4p^3 \times 9p$

d) $3g^4h^3 \times 7g^2h^2$

Solution

a) $2e^4 \times 5e^{10} = (2 \times 5) \times (e^4 \times e^{10}) = 10 \times e^{4+10} = 10e^{14}$

b) $5y^5 \times 3y^3 = (5 \times 3) \times (y^5 \times y^3) = 15 \times y^{5+3} = 15y^8$

c) $4p^3 \times 9p = (4 \times 9) \times (p^3 \times p^1) = 36 \times p^{3+1} = 36p^4$

d) $3g^4h^3 \times 7g^2h^2 = (3 \times 7) \times (g^4 \times g^2) \times (h^3 \times h^2)$
$$= 21 \times g^{4+2} \times h^{3+2}$$
$$= 21g^6h^5$$

Example 3

Use the second rule of indices to simplify:

a) $12p^4 \div 4p^3$

b) $10q^8 \div 5q^6$

c) $8y^5 \div 2y$

d) $6g^5h^5 \div 3g^2h^3$

Solution

a) $12p^4 \div 4p^3 = (12 \div 4) \times (p^4 \div p^3) = 3 \times p^{4-3} = 3p^1 = 3p$

b) $10q^8 \div 5q^6 = (10 \div 5) \times (q^8 \div q^6) = 2 \times q^{8-6} = 2q^2$

c) $8y^5 \div 2y = (8 \div 2) \times (y^5 \div y^1) = 4 \times y^{5-1} = 4y^4$

d) $6g^5h^5 \div 3g^2h^3 = (6 \div 3) \times (g^5 \div g^2) \times (h^5 \div h^3)$
$$= 2 \times g^{5-2} \times h^{5-3}$$
$$= 2g^3h^2$$

Example 4

Remove the brackets in the following expressions.

a) $(3h^3)^2$

b) $(p^3q)^4$

c) $y^2(y^3 + 5y + 1)$

d) $2g(g^2 + 3g - 4)$

Solution

a) $(3h^3)^2 = 3h^3 \times 3h^3 = 9h^{3+3} = 9h^6$

b) $(p^3q)^4 = (p^3)^4 \times q^4 = p^{3\times4} \times q^4 = p^{12}q^4$

c) $y^2(y^3 + 5y + 1) = y^2y^3 + 5y^2y + y^2 = y^5 + 5y^3 + y^2$

d) $2g(g^2 + 3g - 4) = 2gg^2 + 6gg - 8g = 2g^3 + 6g^2 - 8g$

Did you work through the examples with pencil and paper? If not, do that now to make sure that you understand them. Then do the next exercise.

EXERCISE 12

1. Given that $g = 3$ and $h = 4$, calculate the value of:
   a) $5g^4$
   b) g^2h^3
   c) $2g^3 + h^3$
   d) $3h^2 + 2h - 5$

2. Use the first rule of indices to simplify:
   a) $4f^3 \times 3f^4$
   b) $5y^2 \times y^6$
   c) $3e \times 2e^4$
   d) $7pq^2 \times 6p^2q$

3. Use the second rule of indices to simplify:
   a) $8p^8 \div 4p^4$
   b) $7q^5 \div q^4$
   c) $9y^3 \div 3y$
   d) $8p^3q^2 \div 4pq$

4. Remove the brackets in the following expressions.
   a) $(4k^2)^3$
   b) $(3p^4)^2$
   c) $q(3q^2 - 5q - 1)$
   d) $5y^4(y^2 + 2y - 7)$

Check your answers at the end of this module.

B Zero and negative indices

We have already said that a^n is shorthand for $a \times a \times a \times \ldots$ (to n factors). This definition only makes sense if n is a positive whole number. This means that, for example, a^0 and a^{-3} have no meaning at the moment.

Mathematicians always prefer to have rules, formulae and patterns which apply in all situations – they hate exceptions to their rules! So let me show you how to find the rules for a^0 and $a^{-\text{number}}$.

Look at $a^3 \div a^3$. No matter what number 'a' stands for, the value of $a^3 \div a^3$ is 1 because a number divided by itself is 1 (unless a is zero – we cannot divide zero by zero).

If we use the second rule of indices, $a^3 \div a^3 = a^{3-3} = a^0$. So a^0 must be 1.

$$a^0 = 1 \text{ for all values of } a \text{ except } a = 0$$

Although it may seem strange at first, this means that $2^0 = 1$, $3^0 = 1$, $(\frac{1}{2})^0 = 1$ and also $(1\,000\,000)^0 = 1$.

Let us now consider the value of $a^2 \div a^5$.

We can work this out as follows: $a^2 \div a^5 = \dfrac{a \times a}{a \times a \times a \times a \times a}$

$$= \dfrac{1}{a \times a \times a}$$

$$= \dfrac{1}{a^3}$$

If you use the second rule of indices

$$a^2 \div a^5 = a^{2-5} = a^{-3}$$

so a^{-3} is a shorthand form of $\frac{1}{a^3}$.

In other words, a^{-3} is the *reciprocal* of a^3. Once again, a must not be zero because we cannot divide by 0.

$$a^{-n} = \tfrac{1}{a^n} \text{ (the reciprocal of } a^n) \text{ except when } a = 0$$

You need lots of practice to get used to these new ideas so work through these examples with me:

Example 1

Find the value of:

a) 2^{-3}

b) 21^0

c) $(\frac{2}{3})^{-4}$

d) $3^0 \times 3^2 \times 3^4$

Solution

a) $2^{-3} = \frac{1}{2^3} = \frac{1}{8}$

b) $21^0 = 1$

c) $(\frac{2}{3})^{-4} = (\frac{3}{2})^4 = \frac{81}{16}$

d) $3^0 \times 3^2 \times 3^4 = 3^{0+2+4} = 3^6 = 729$

Example 2

Simplify:

a) $p^3 \times p^5 \times p^{-2}$

b) $q^{-4} \times q \times q^2$

c) $e^2 \div e^5$

d) $f^{-2} \times f^2$

Solution

a) $p^3 \times p^5 \times p^{-2} = p^{3+5+(-2)} = p^6$

b) $q^{-4} \times q \times q^2 = q^{-4} \times q^1 \times q^2 = q^{(-4)+1+2} = q^{-1}$

c) $e^2 \div e^5 = e^{2-5} = e^{-3}$

d) $f^{-2} \times f^2 = f^{(-2)+2} = f^0 = 1$

Example 3

Simplify:

a) $y^5 \div y^3$

b) $y^5 \times y^{-3}$

c) $((\frac{3}{4})^{-1})^{-1}$

d) $k^5 \div k^{-2}$

Solution

a) $y^5 \div y^3 = y^{5-3} = y^2$

b) $y^5 \times y^{-3} = y^{5 + (-3)} = y^2$

c) $(\frac{3}{4})^{-1}$ is the reciprocal of $\frac{3}{4}$ so it is $\frac{4}{3}$.

$(\frac{4}{3})^{-1}$ is the reciprocal of $\frac{4}{3}$ so it is $\frac{3}{4}$. Hence $((\frac{3}{4})^{-1})^{-1} = \frac{3}{4}$.

d) $k^5 \div k^{-2} = k^5 \times k^2$

$= k^{5 + 2}$ | dividing by k^{-2} is the same as multiplying by its

$= k^7$ | reciprocal k^2

Or: $k^5 \div k^{-2} = k^{5-(-2)}$

$= k^{5 + 2}$

$= k^7$

EXERCISE 13

1. Find the value of:

    a) $(5)^{-2}$

    b) $(0.0006)^0$

    c) $(\frac{2}{5})^{-3}$

    d) $4^{-1} \times 4^0 \times 4^3$

2. Simplify:

    a) $y^6 \times y^{-2}$

    b) $k^5 \times k \times k^{-6}$

    c) $p^3 \div p^6$

    d) $q^4 \div q^{-2}$

3. Simplify:

    a) $e^6 \div e^2$

    b) $e^6 \div e^{-2}$

    c) $(2^{-1})^{-1}$

    d) $k \div k^{-3}$

Check your answers at the end of this module.

Using your calculator for indices

In some calculators the y^x or x^y is not on a key – it is written *above* the key. If your calculator is like that then you must press the

SHIFT key or 2ndF key each time before you press that key below y^x or x^y.

Look at the keys on your calculator and find the one marked y^x or x^y. This key can be used to work out expressions involving indices.

Here are some examples:

To work out 2^8 press the keys [2] [y^x] [8] [=]. You get the answer 256.

To work out 3^7 press the keys [3] [y^x] [7] [=]. You get the answer 2187.

To work out 4^{-3} press the keys [4] [y^x] [3] [+/−] [=]. You get the answer 0.015625.

To work out $6^7 \div 5^4$ press the keys

[6] [y^x] [7] [=] [÷] [5] [y^x] [4] [=] .

You get the answer 447.8976.

To work out 9876×8^{-5} press the keys

[9] [8] [7] [6] [×] [8] [y^x] [5] [+/−] [=] .

You get the answer 0.301391601.

Now use your calculator to check the following results:
$5^9 = 1953125$
$(3.5)^6 = 1838.265625$
$3^{-4} = 0.012345679$
$8^5 \times 3^6 = 23887872$
$8^5 \div 3^6 = 44.94924554$
$7^5 \times 4^{-6} = 4.103271484$

C Writing numbers in standard form

In science, and in other subjects, you often have to deal with very large and very small numbers. For example, the distance from Jupiter to the sun is 778 000 000 km and the wavelength of green light is 0.0000005 m. It is very difficult to compare numbers or to calculate with numbers in this form. Sometimes we try to overcome the difficulty by talking about large numbers in 'millions' or 'billions', and talking about small numbers in 'millionths'.

A more useful method is to use **standard form** (sometimes called **scientific notation**).

We can easily express numbers such as 1000, 1 000 000 and 1 000 000 000 as powers of 10:

$$1000 = 10 \times 10 \times 10 = 10^3$$
$$1\ 000\ 000 = 10 \times 10 \times 10 \times 10 \times 10 \times 10 = 10^6$$
$$1\ 000\ 000\ 000 = 10 \times 10 \times 10 \times 10 \times 10 \times 10 \times 10 \times 10 \times 10 = 10^9$$

Other numbers can be expressed as a product of two factors, one of which is a power of 10 and the other a number between 1 and 10.

For example, $700\,000 = 7 \times 100\,000 = 7 \times 10^5$
                    $2\,500\,000 = 2.5 \times 1\,000\,000 = 2.5 \times 10^6$
                    $876\,000\,000 = 8.76 \times 100\,000\,000 = 8.76 \times 10^8$

A number written in this way is in **standard form**.

> The standard form of a number is $a \times 10^n$ where n is an integer and $1 \leqslant a < 10$

Here are some more examples:

The standard form of 1234 is 1.234×10^3.
The standard form of 456.7 is 4.567×10^2.
The standard form of 9 500 000 is 9.5×10^6.

Notice that the power of 10 gives the **order of magnitude** of the number. For example,

1234 is in the 'thousands' and 10^3 is a thousand
456.7 is in the 'hundreds' and 10^2 is a hundred
9 500 000 is in the 'millions' and 10^6 is a million

Notice also that to change 1234 to 1.234 (so that it is between 1 and 10), the decimal point is moved *three* places to the *left*, and *three* is the index of the 10.

To change 456.7 to 4.567 (so that it is between 1 and 10), the decimal point is moved *two* places to the *left*, and *two* is the index of the 10.

Now look at these numbers:

$0.432 = 4.32 \div 10 = 4.32 \times 10^{-1}$
The standard form of 0.432 is 4.32×10^{-1}.
$0.0095 = 9.5 \div 10^3 = 9.5 \times 10^{-3}$
The standard form of 0.0095 is 9.5×10^{-3}.

Numbers less than 1 have a negative index on the 10 in their standard form.

0.432 is four and a bit 'tenths' and 10^{-1} is a tenth
0.0095 is nine and a bit 'thousandths' and 10^{-3} is a thousandth

To change 0.432 to 4.32 (so that it is between 1 and 10), the decimal point is moved *one* place to the *right*, and *minus one* is the index on the 10.

To change 0.0095 to 9.5 (so that it is between 1 and 10), the decimal point is moved *three* places to the *right*, and *minus three* is the index on the 10.

To complete this work we should consider the standard form of numbers between 1 and 10. In this case, the decimal point does not need to be moved to obtain the value of 'a' and so the index on the 10 is zero.

For example, the standard form of 3.142 is 3.142×10^0. This makes sense because, as you already know, $10^0 = 1$.

Examples

Express the following in standard form.
a)   3579.2
b)   1 020 304
c)   0.000461
d)   0.000001

> remember to count how many places you move the decimal point to the left or right to work out the index on the 10

Solutions

a) $3579.2 = 3.5792 \times 10^3$
b) $1\ 020\ 304 = 1.020304 \times 10^6$
c) $0.000461 = 4.61 \times 10^{-4}$
d) $0.000001 = 1 \times 10^{-6}$

Multiplying and dividing numbers in standard form

Work through the examples, remembering the rules for working with indices.

Example 1

Work out the value of the following, giving your answers in standard form.
a) $(2.5 \times 10^5) \times (3.12 \times 10^7)$
b) $(5 \times 10^3) \times (1.24 \times 10^{-6})$
c) $(9.5 \times 10^4) \times (7.3 \times 10^2)$
d) $(3.45 \times 10^{-3}) \times (8 \times 10^{-2})$

Solution

a) $(2.5 \times 10^5) \times (3.12 \times 10^7) = (2.5 \times 3.12) \times (10^5 \times 10^7) = 7.8 \times 10^{12}$
b) $(5 \times 10^3) \times (1.24 \times 10^{-6}) = (5 \times 1.24) \times (10^3 \times 10^{-6}) = 6.2 \times 10^{-3}$
c) $(9.5 \times 10^4) \times (7.3 \times 10^2) = 69.35 \times 10^6$
     69.35 is not between 1 and 10, so we change it to 6.935×10^1
     and the result of the calculation $= (6.935 \times 10^1) \times 10^6$
     $$= 6.935 \times 10^7$$
d) $(3.45 \times 10^{-3}) \times (8 \times 10^{-2}) = 27.6 \times 10^{-5}$
     $$= (2.76 \times 10^1) \times 10^{-5}$$
     $$= 2.76 \times 10^{-4}$$

Example 2

Work out the value of the following, giving your answers in standard form.
a) $(8.5 \times 10^6) \div (5 \times 10^2)$
b) $(6 \times 10^5) \div (4 \times 10^{-3})$
c) $(2 \times 10^8) \div (5 \times 10^5)$
d) $(1.5 \times 10^{-2}) \div (4 \times 10^{-6})$

Solution

a) $(8.5 \times 10^6) \div (5 \times 10^2) = (8.5 \div 5) \times (10^6 \div 10^2)$
     $= 1.7 \times 10^4$
b) $(6 \times 10^5) \div (4 \times 10^{-3}) = (6 \div 4) \times (10^5 \div 10^{-3)}$
     $$= 1.5 \times 10^{5-(-3)}$$
     $$= 1.5 \times 10^8$$

c) $(2 \times 10^8) \div (5 \times 10^5) = 0.4 \times 10^3$
0.4 is not between 1 and 10, so we change it to 4×10^{-1}
and the result of the calculation $= (4 \times 10^{-1}) \times 10^3$
$$= 4 \times 10^2$$

d) $(1.5 \times 10^{-2}) \div (4 \times 10^{-6}) = 0.375 \times 10^{-2-(-6)}$
$$= 0.375 \times 10^{-2+6}$$
$$= 0.375 \times 10^4$$
$$= (3.75 \times 10^{-1}) \times 10^4$$
$$= 3.75 \times 10^3$$

Adding and subtracting numbers in standard form

The rules of indices only apply to multiplications and divisions. There are no rules for additions and subtractions.

If the powers of 10 are the same, addition and subtraction are straightforward. But, if the powers are not the same, the easiest method is to change the numbers from their standard form to their ordinary form. The following examples will make the method clear.

Example 1

Work out the value of the following, giving your answers in standard form:

a) $(3.2 \times 10^5) + (6.5 \times 10^5)$
b) $(7.23 \times 10^3) + (4.8 \times 10^3)$
c) $(4.8 \times 10^5) + (7.3 \times 10^3)$
d) $(6 \times 10^{-1}) + (9 \times 10^{-2})$

Solution

a) $(3.2 \times 10^5) + (6.5 \times 10^5) = (3.2 + 6.5) \times 10^5$
$$= 9.7 \times 10^5$$

b) $(7.23 \times 10^3) + (4.8 \times 10^3) = 12.03 \times 10^3$
$$= (1.203 \times 10^1) \times 10^3$$
$$= 1.203 \times 10^4$$

c) $(4.8 \times 10^5) + (7.3 \times 10^3) = (480\ 000) + (7300)$
$$= 487\ 300$$
$$= 4.873 \times 10^5$$

d) $(6 \times 10^{-1}) + (9 \times 10^{-2}) = (0.6) + (0.09)$
$$= 0.69$$
$$= 6.9 \times 10^{-1}$$

Example 2

Work out the values of the following, giving your answers in standard form.

a) $(7.25 \times 10^4) - (2.8 \times 10^4)$
b) $(4.6 \times 10^{-2}) - (1.32 \times 10^{-2})$
c) $(8 \times 10^3) - (3.9 \times 10^{-1})$
d) $(1.75 \times 10^4) - (7.32 \times 10^3)$

Solution

a) $(7.25 \times 10^4) - (2.8 \times 10^4) = (7.25 - 2.8) \times 10^4 = 4.45 \times 10^4$

b) $(4.6 \times 10^{-2}) - (1.32 \times 10^{-2}) = (4.6 - 1.32) \times 10^{-2} = 3.28 \times 10^{-2}$

c) $(8 \times 10^3) - (3.9 \times 10^{-1}) = (8000) - (0.39)$
$$= 7999.61$$
$$= 7.99961 \times 10^3$$

d) $(1.75 \times 10^4) - (7.32 \times 10^3) = (17500) - (7320)$
$$= 10180$$
$$= 1.0180 \times 10^4$$

Using your calculator for standard form calculations

If there is a key on your calculator marked $\boxed{\text{EXP}}$, you can use it to do calculations with numbers in standard form.

To enter the number 5.6×10^4 in the calculator, press the keys

.

The display on the calculator will be $\boxed{5.6 \quad ^{04}}$.

To enter the number 7×10^{-3} in the calculator, press the keys

.

The display on the calculator will be $\boxed{7. \quad ^{-03}}$.

Examples and solutions

1.   To do the multiplication $(3.4 \times 10^5) \times (7.6 \times 10^8)$, press the keys

.

The calculator shows $\boxed{2.584 \quad ^{14}}$ which means

the answer is 2.584×10^{14}.

2.   To do the addition $(5.67 \times 10^5) + (8.5 \times 10^3)$, press the keys

.

The calculator shows $\boxed{575500}$. If the answer is required in standard form, you must change 575500 to 5.755×10^5.

3.   To do the division $(3.85 \times 10^5) \div (5.5 \times 10^{-3})$, press the keys

.

The calculator shows $\boxed{70000000}$ which in standard form is 7×10^7.

It is time that you tested your understanding of the work we have done on standard form. I recommend that you answer some of the questions without using a calculator, but you should also do some questions with your calculator to discover whether you have understood the use of the $\boxed{\text{EXP}}$ button.

EXERCISE 14

1. Express the following in standard form.
   a) 78900
   b) 347.9
   c) 0.000058
   d) 0.1234

2. Write the following numbers in their ordinary form.
   a) 1.2×10^2
   b) 3.14×10^{-2}
   c) 7.605×10^{-4}
   d) 2.8×10^9

3. Work out the following, giving your answers in standard form.
   a) $(4 \times 10^4) \times (1.2 \times 10^6)$
   b) $(2.4 \times 10^8) \times (6 \times 10^{-5})$
   c) $(5.6 \times 10^6) \div (3.5 \times 10^2)$
   d) $(1.25 \times 10^4) \div (2.5 \times 10^{-7})$
   e) $(6.9 \times 10^5) + (3.8 \times 10^4)$
   f) $(9 \times 10^{-1}) + (8.3 \times 10^{-2})$
   g) $(2.7 \times 10^4) - (4.3 \times 10^3)$
   h) $(8.5 \times 10^{-2}) - (7 \times 10^{-4})$

Practical problems with numbers in standard form

Example 1

Jupiter is 778 000 000 km from the sun.
a) Write 778 000 000 in standard form.
b) Light travels at a speed of 3.00×10^5 km/s.
   Calculate the time, correct to the nearest minute, that light takes to travel from the sun to Jupiter.

Solution

a) $778\ 000\ 000 = 7.78 \times 100\ 000\ 000 = 7.78 \times 10^8$
b) Time for light to travel from the sun to Jupiter

   $= \dfrac{\text{distance}}{\text{speed}}$

   $= \dfrac{7.78 \times 10^8 \text{ km}}{3.00 \times 10^5 \text{ km/s}}$

   $= 2.593 \times 10^3$ seconds

   $= 2593$ seconds
   $= 2593 \div 60$ to change seconds into minutes you divide by 60
   $= 43$ minutes (to the nearest minute)

Example 2

In 1985 the population of the Soviet Union was 2.70×10^8 and the population of China was 1.02×10^9. Calculate the total population of the Soviet Union and China in 1985. Give your answer in standard form.

Solution

$$\text{Total population} = (2.7 \times 10^8) + (1.02 \times 10^9)$$
$$= (270\ 000\ 000) + (1\ 020\ 000\ 000)$$
$$= 1\ 290\ 000\ 000$$
$$= 1.29 \times 10^9$$

Example 3

The mass of the moon is 7.35×10^{22} kg and the mass of the earth is 5.98×10^{24} kg. Express the mass of the moon as a percentage of the mass of the earth, giving your answer correct to 3 significant figures.

Solution

$$\frac{\text{mass of the moon}}{\text{mass of the earth}} = \frac{7.35 \times 10^{22}}{5.98 \times 10^{24}}$$
$$= 1.229 \times 10^{-2}$$
$$= 1.229 \times \frac{1}{100} \times \frac{100}{100}$$
$$= 1.23\% \text{ to 3 significant figures.}$$

Example 4

A glacier moves at 3.2×10^{-7} km/h. Calculate how far it moves in a year. (Take a year to be 365 days.)

Solution

$$\text{Number of hours in 1 year} = 24 \times 365$$
$$\text{Distance glacier moves in 1 year} = 3.2 \times 10^{-7} \times 24 \times 365 \text{ km}$$
$$= 28\ 032 \times 10^{-7} \text{ km}$$
$$= (2.8032 \times 10^4) \times 10^{-7} \text{ km}$$
$$= 2.8032 \times 10^{-3} \text{ km}$$
$$= 2.8032 \times \frac{1}{1000} \times 1000 \text{ m}$$
$$= 2.8032 \text{ m}$$

Now try a few problems on your own to see if you have a good grasp of the work on standard form.

EXERCISE 15

1. The distance from the sun to the earth is 1.496×10^8 km. Light travels at 2.998×10^5 km/s. Calculate the time, to the nearest second, that it takes light to travel from the sun to the earth.
2. The area of Portugal is 9.191×10^4 km^2 and the area of Spain is 4.9259×10^5 km^2. Calculate the total area of Portugal and Spain in square kilometres.

3. The diameter of a red blood cell is 7.14×10^{-4} cm and the diameter of a white blood cell is 1.243×10^{-3} cm. Calculate the difference, in centimetres, between these two diameters. Give your answer in standard form.

4. The area of South Africa is 1.2247×10^6 km^2 and in 1995 there were, on average, 33.67 people per square kilometre. Calculate the population of South Africa in 1995, giving your answer in standard form.

Check your answers at the end of this module.

Learners following the CORE syllabus should now turn to the 'Summary' before doing the 'Check your progress', at the end of Section D. Learners following the EXTENDED syllabus should study the section on fractional indices first.

D Fractional indices

We now know the meaning of a^n when the index n is a positive whole number, a negative whole number or zero. We still have no meaning for expressions such as $9^{\frac{1}{2}}$, $8^{-\frac{2}{3}}$ and $(32)^{0.4}$.

As before, our definitions of such expressions must fit in with the rules of indices.

Let us first consider $a^{\frac{1}{2}}$. If we multiply it by itself using the first rule of indices, we get $a^{\frac{1}{2}} \times a^{\frac{1}{2}} = a^{\frac{1}{2}+\frac{1}{2}} = a^1 = a$. In other words the square of $a^{\frac{1}{2}}$ is a, so $a^{\frac{1}{2}}$ must be the square root of a.

$$(a^{\frac{1}{2}})^2 = a, \text{ so } a^{\frac{1}{2}} = \sqrt{a}$$

Similarly, $a^{\frac{1}{3}} \times a^{\frac{1}{3}} \times a^{\frac{1}{3}} = a^{\frac{1}{3}+\frac{1}{3}+\frac{1}{3}} = a^1 = a$

so the cube of $a^{\frac{1}{3}}$ is a.

So $a^{\frac{1}{3}}$ is the cube root of a. $$(a^{\frac{1}{3}})^3 = a, \text{ so } a^{\frac{1}{3}} = \sqrt[3]{a}$$

$$a^{\frac{1}{n}} \text{ is the } n^{\text{th}} \text{ root of a or } a^{\frac{1}{n}} = \sqrt[n]{a}$$

To interpret other fractional powers, we use the third rule of indices.
$$a^{\frac{m}{n}} = a^{m \times \frac{(1)}{n}} = [a^m]^{\frac{1}{n}} = \sqrt[n]{a^m}$$
Alternatively, $a^{\frac{m}{n}} = a^{\frac{1}{n} \times m} = [a^{\frac{1}{n}}]^m = (\sqrt[n]{a})^m$.

If the index is a decimal, we must change it to a fraction in order to interpret it. For example,
$$a^{0.4} = a^{\frac{4}{10}} = a^{\frac{2}{5}} = \sqrt[5]{a^2}$$

If the index is negative, we must remember that a^{-1} stands for $\frac{1}{a}$, that is the reciprocal of a.

A few examples should make this clear to you.

Example 1

Work out the value of:

a) $9^{\frac{1}{2}}$

b) $8^{\frac{2}{3}}$

c) $36^{\frac{3}{2}}$

d) $81^{0.75}$

Solution

a) $9^{\frac{1}{2}} = \sqrt{9} = 3$ (Notice that we take the *positive* square root.)

b) $8^{\frac{2}{3}} = (\sqrt[3]{8})^2 = (2)^2 = 4$

c) $36^{\frac{3}{2}} = (\sqrt{36})^3 = (6)^3 = 216$

d) $81^{0.75} = 81^{\frac{3}{4}} = (\sqrt[4]{81})^3 = (3)^3 = 27$

Example 2

Work out the value of:

a) $(\frac{16}{25})^{\frac{3}{2}}$

b) $4^{\frac{1}{6}} \times 4^{\frac{1}{3}}$

c) $8^{\frac{5}{6}} \div 8^{\frac{1}{2}}$

d) $32^{0.2}$

Solution

a) $(\frac{16}{25})^{\frac{3}{2}} = (\sqrt{\frac{16}{25}})^3 = (\frac{4}{5})^3 = \frac{64}{125}$

b) $4^{\frac{1}{6}} \times 4^{\frac{1}{3}} = 4^{(\frac{1}{6}) + (\frac{1}{3})} = 4^{\frac{1}{2}} = \sqrt{4} = 2$

c) $8^{\frac{5}{6}} \div 8^{\frac{1}{2}} = 8^{(\frac{5}{6}) - (\frac{1}{2})} = 8^{\frac{1}{3}} = \sqrt[3]{8} = 2$

d) $32^{0.2} = 32^{\frac{1}{5}} = \sqrt[5]{32} = 2$

Example 3

Simplify:

a) $64^{-\frac{2}{3}}$

b) $(\frac{4}{9})^{-\frac{5}{2}}$

c) $e^{\frac{3}{4}} \div e^{-\frac{5}{4}}$

d) $(f^{\frac{1}{3}})^{\frac{1}{2}}$

Solution

a) $64^{-\frac{2}{3}} = (\frac{1}{64})^{\frac{2}{3}} = (\sqrt[3]{\frac{1}{64}})^2 = (\frac{1}{4})^2 = \frac{1}{16}$

b) $(\frac{4}{9})^{-\frac{5}{2}} = (\frac{9}{4})^{\frac{5}{2}} = (\sqrt{\frac{9}{4}})^5 = (\frac{3}{2})^5 = \frac{243}{32}$

c) $e^{\frac{3}{4}} \div e^{-\frac{5}{4}} = e^{(\frac{3}{4}) - (-\frac{5}{4})} = e^{\frac{8}{4}} = e^2$

d) $(f^{\frac{1}{3}})^{\frac{1}{2}} = f^{\frac{1}{3} \times \frac{1}{2}} = f^{\frac{1}{6}} = \sqrt[6]{f}$

Now, here are a few questions for you to try.

EXERCISE 16

1. Work out the value of:
   a) $16^{\frac{1}{2}}$
   b) $27^{\frac{2}{3}}$
   c) $25^{\frac{3}{2}}$
   d) $10\ 000^{0.75}$

2. Work out the value of:
   a) $(\frac{25}{4})^{\frac{3}{2}}$
   b) $8^{\frac{1}{4}} \times 8^{\frac{1}{12}}$
   c) $9^{\frac{3}{4}} \div 9^{\frac{1}{4}}$
   d) $32^{0.6}$

3. Simplify:
   a) $27^{-\frac{2}{3}}$
   b) $(\frac{9}{25})^{-\frac{3}{2}}$
   c) $e^{-\frac{1}{2}} \div e^{-\frac{3}{2}}$
   d) $(f^{\frac{1}{2}})^6$

Check your answers at the end of this module.

Summary

So now you've come to the end of this unit. Well done if you feel comfortable working with indices. If you don't it's probably because you don't know the rules well and you're getting confused. You must make sure you understand them before you continue. So go over them again and practise some more if you need to before you continue with the next unit. These are the rules for working with indices that you should remember:

- $a^m \times a^n = a^{m + n}$
- $a^m \div a^n = a^{m - n}$
- $(a^m)^n = a^{mn}$
- $a^\circ = 1$
- $a^{-n} = \frac{1}{a^n}$
- $a^{\frac{1}{n}} = \sqrt[n]{a}$

You should also remember that:

- the standard form of a number is $a \times 10^n$ where n is an integer and a is a number between 1 and 10.

You're going to be looking at working with positive and negative numbers again in the next unit. This time you'll be multiplying and dividing as well as adding and subtracting. You'll need these skills to help you with the algebra in the unit.

Check your progress

1. Work out the value of:
   a) $4^3 \times 5^2$
   b) $2^6 + 2^3 + 2^0$
   c) $5^{-1} + 5^{-2}$
   d) $(6 \times 10^8) \div (2 \times 10^6)$

2. a) Complete the statement below by putting the symbol $<$ or $>$ between the numbers.
      $33.8 \times 10^4 \qquad 2.7 \times 10^6$
   b) Which of the above two numbers is written in standard form?
   c) Rewrite the other number in standard form.

3. Simplify:
   a) $33p^2 \div 11p^{-4}$
   b) $(5q^{12})^2$
   c) $2y^2 \times 3y^{-5}$

4. A heart beats once every second. How many times will the heart beat in a lifetime of 70 years? Take a year to be 365.25 days and give your answer in standard form.

5. A square centimetre of high resolution photographic film holds 1.5×10^8 bits of information. A large encyclopedia holds 4×10^{10} bits of information.
   What area of high resolution film is needed to hold all the information from the encyclopedia? Give your answer correct to 3 significant figures.

6. a) Simplify:
      (i) $(16e^{10})^{-\frac{1}{2}}$
      (ii) $2p^{\frac{1}{2}} \times 3p^{-\frac{5}{2}}$
   b) Find the value of x which satisfies:
      (i) $3^x = 81$
      (ii) $3^x = \frac{1}{9}$
      (iii) $3^x = 1$

Algebraic Manipulation

If you've been feeling a little unsure about working with positive and negative numbers you'll be able to get more practice now. I'm starting this unit by reminding you about how to work with these numbers (remember the number line?). You'll need to be very comfortable with these ideas when you get to the algebra work in this unit where you'll be working with algebraic expressions.

This unit has four sections:

Section	Title	Time
A	Working with directed numbers	3 hours
B	Simplifying algebraic expressions	2 hours
C	Factorising algebraic expressions	3 hours
D	Transforming more complicated formulae	2 hours

By the end of this unit you should be able to:

- do calculations involving directed numbers
- remove brackets and simplify algebraic expressions
- factorise algebraic expressions
- manipulate algebraic fractions
- transform more complicated formulae.

A Working with directed numbers

You will remember that, in Module 1, you learnt about positive and negative numbers. Before you do any new work. I'll refresh your memories about adding.

Here is a number line.

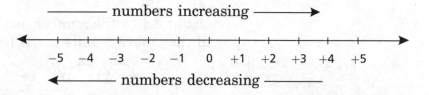

Positive and negative numbers are called **directed numbers**. Zero is neither positive nor negative. The numbers increase as you move to the right on the number line, and they decrease as you move to the left. Directed numbers can be whole numbers or fractions or decimal numbers. Can you see that

$-4.6 < -4$, $+\frac{1}{2} > -\frac{1}{2}$ and $-100 < +0.005$?

Whole directed numbers are called **integers**, so the set of integers is $(\ldots, -4, -3, -2, -1, 0, +1, +2, +3, +4, \ldots)$.

Addition and subtraction of directed numbers

This is revision – you may remember that, in Module 1, you learnt how to deal with increases, decreases and differences of temperature (which are directed numbers). You may feel confident that you can add and subtract directed numbers without any trouble. If so, you should read quickly through the examples and then answer the questions in Exercise 17.

If you are not so confident, you should work through the examples carefully before tackling the exercise.

Example 1

Work out:
a) $(+2) + (+5)$ b) $(-2) + (+6)$ c) $(+4) + (-5)$
d) $(-1) + (-3)$ e) $(+2) + (-2)$

> Remember that when you work on the number line ' + ' means move right and ' − ' means move left.

Solution

a) To use the number line to work out $(+2) + (+5)$ start at $+2$ on the number line and then move 5 units to the right.

$+(+5)$ means move *right* 5 places

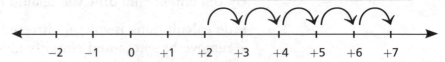

So the result is $(+2) + (+5) = (+7)$.

b) $(-2) + (+6)$
Start at -2 on the number line and move 6 units to the right.

$+(+6)$ means move *right* 6 places

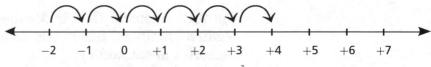

So $(-2) + (+6) = (+4)$.

c) $(+4) + (-5)$
Start at $+4$ on the number line and then move 5 units to the left.

$+(-5)$ means move *left* 5 places

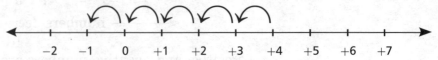

You can see that $(+4) + (-5) = (-1)$.

d) $(-1) + (-3)$
Start at -1 on the number line and then move 3 units to the left.

$+(-3)$ means move *left* 3 places

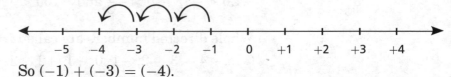

So $(-1) + (-3) = (-4)$.

e) $(+2) + (-2)$
Start at $+2$ on the number line
and then move 2 units to the left.

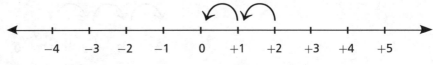

$+(-2)$ means move *left* 2 places

So $(+2) + (-2) = 0$.

Example 2

Work out:
a) $(+2) - (-5)$ b) $(-2) - (-6)$ c) $(+4) - (+5)$
d) $(-1) - (+3)$ e) $(+2) - (+2)$

Solution

a) $(+2) - (-5)$
Start at $+2$ on the number line. If the sum was $(+2) + (-5)$ you
would move 5 places to the left. But the sum is $(+2) - (-5)$ so you
must move 5 places to the right.

$-(-5)$ means move *right* 2 places

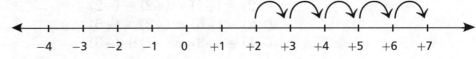

So $(+2) - (-5) = (+7)$.
Notice that $(+2) - (-5) = (+2) + (+5) = (+7)$.

b) $(-2) - (-6)$
Start at -2 on the number line. If it was $(-2) + (-6)$ you would
move 6 places to the left. So $(-2) - (-6)$ must mean move 6
places to the right.

$-(-6)$ means move *right* 6 places

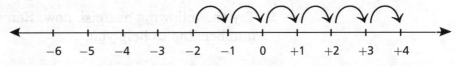

So $(-2) - (-6) = (-2) + (+6) = (+4)$.

c) $(+4) - (+5)$ is the same as $(+4) + (-5)$.
Start at $+4$ and move
5 places to the left.

$-(+5)$ means move *left* 5 places

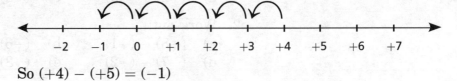

So $(+4) - (+5) = (-1)$

d) $(-1) - (+3)$ is the same as $(-1) + (-3)$.
    Start at -1 and move 3 places
    to the left.

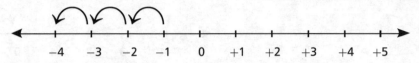

So $(-1) - (+3) = (-4)$

e) $(+2) - (+2)$ is the same as $(+2) + (-2)$.
    Start at $+2$ and move 2 places
    to the left.

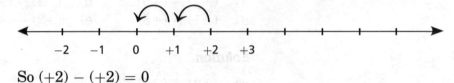

So $(+2) - (+2) = 0$

Look carefully at the examples again. Compare the results from
Example 1 and Example 2. Notice the following:

$(+2) - (-5) = (+2) + (+5)$
$(+4) - (+5) = (+4) + (-5)$
$(+2) - (+2) = (+2) + (-2)$
$(-2) - (-6) = (-2) + (+6)$
$(-1) - (+3) = (-1) + (-3)$

To summarise:

subtracting a negative number is the same as adding a positive number
subtracting a positive number is the same as adding a negative number

This means that you can change subtractions into additions like this:

$(-5) - (-3) = (-5) + (+3) = (-2)$
$(+9) - (-7) = (+9) + (+7) = (+16)$
$(-8) - (+6) = (-8) + (-6) = (-14)$
$(+4) - (+2) = (+4) + (-2) = (+2)$

Try the following exercise now. Remember to draw yourself a
number line to help you.

EXERCISE 17

1. Work out:
    a) $(+3) + (+6)$ b) $(-4) + (+3)$ c) $(+7) + (-5)$
    d) $(-2) + (-5)$ e) $(-3) + (-3)$

2. Work out:
    a) $(+8) - (+1)$ b) $(+6) - (-4)$ c) $(-2) - (+1)$
    d) $(-7) - (-2)$ e) $(-3) - (-12)$

3. Work out:
    a) $(+2) + (+3) + (+4)$ b) $(-6) + (+5) - (-7)$
    c) $(-1) - (+8) + (+2)$ d) $(+4) - (-9) - (-6)$

Check your answers at the end of this module.

Multiplication of directed numbers

No doubt you will have noticed that, as far as addition and subtraction are concerned, positive directed numbers behave in the same way as ordinary numbers (whole, fractional and decimal).

For example, $(+2) + (+5) = (+7)$ and $2 + 5 = 7$
$(+3) + (+6) = (+9)$ and $3 + 6 = 9$
$(+8) - (+1) = (+7)$ and $8 - 1 = 7$
$(+2) - (+2) = 0$ and $2 - 2 = 0$
$(+2) + (+3) + (+4) = (+9)$ and $2 + 3 + 4 = 9$
$(+5.5) - (+2.4) = (+3.1)$ and $5.5 - 2.4 = 3.1$

For this reason, positive directed numbers are often written without the '+' sign. We usually write temperature as, for example, $20°C$ instead of $+20°C$.

When we consider multiplication involving positive directed numbers, we must have the same rules as for ordinary numbers.

So, we say that $(+2) \times (+5) = (+10)$ to match $2 \times 5 = 10$.

In general, $(+a) \times (+b) = (+ab)$ and (positive) × (positive) = (positive). When we have, for example, $(-3) \times (+2)$, we compare it with $(-3) \times 2$.
$(-3) \times 2$ we can interpret as $(-3) + (-3)$, which is (-6).
We say that $(-3) \times (+2) = (-6)$ to match $(-3) \times 2 = (-6)$.

In general $(-a) \times (+b) = (-ab)$ and (negative) × (positive) = (negative).

For ordinary numbers, $a \times b = b \times a$. So we shall want $(+2) \times (-3)$ to have the same value as $(-3) \times (+2)$. This means that, in general, $(+a) \times (-b) = (-ab)$ and (positive) × (negative) = (negative).

The last case we have to consider is $(-a) \times (-b)$. There is no rule involving ordinary numbers which will help us to decide what (negative) × (negative) should be. However, we have met such a situation when we were dealing with indices.

The second rule of indices gave us the result $a^{-1} = \frac{1}{a}$ and so $(a^{-1})^{-1} = (\frac{1}{a})^{-1} = \frac{a}{1} = a^1$ so $(a^{-1})^{-1} = a^1$ and since the third rule of indices is $(a^m)^n = a^{(m \times n)}$ it follows that $(-1) \times (-1) = 1$ so we can write $(-1) \times (-1) = (+1)$.

Hence, $(-a) \times (-b) = (-1) \times a \times (-1) \times b = (-1) \times (-1) \times a \times b$
$= (+ab)$.
In general, $(-a) \times (-b) = (+ab)$ and (negative) × (negative) = (positive).

To summarise, what you need to remember when multiplying directed numbers:

> (positive) × (positive) = (positive)
> (positive) × (negative) = (negative)
> (negative) × (positive) = (negative)
> (negative) × (negative) = (positive)

You could remember this by saying

'two like signs give positive; two unlike signs give negative'

but you have to remember that you are talking about *multiplication* and not addition!

If you have to multiply more than two numbers together, you need to think about how many of them are negative.

If two of them are negative, the answer is positive.
If three of them are negative, the answer is negative.
If four of them are negative, the answer is positive.
If five of them are negative, the answer is negative.

In fact if the number of negative numbers is even, the answer is positive and if the number of negative numbers is odd, the answer is negative.

Example 1

Work out:

a) $(-6) \times (+2) \times (-4)$　　　　　b) $(-2)^5$

c) $2 \times (-3) \times (-5)^2$

Solution

a) $6 \times 2 \times 4 = 48$ and there are two negative numbers multiplied together, so $(-6) \times (+2) \times (-4) = (+48)$.

b) $(-2)^5$ means $(-2) \times (-2) \times (-2) \times (-2) \times (-2)$ so there are five negative numbers multiplied together.
Hence $(-2)^5 = (-32)$.

c) $2 \times (-3) \times (-5)^2$ means $2 \times (-3) \times (-5) \times (-5)$ so there are three negative numbers multiplied together.
Hence $2 \times (-3) \times (-5)^2 = (-150)$.

Example 2

Given that $p = 5$, $q = -2$ and $r\ -3$, work out the value of:

a) $8pq$　　　　　　b) qr^3

c) $p^3 + q^3$　　　　　d) $p^2 - 4qr$

Solution

a) $8pq = 8 \times 5 \times (-2) = (-80)$

b) $qr^3 = (-2) \times (-3) \times (-3) \times (-3)$ 　　　| only the r is cubed |
$\quad = (+54)$

c) $p^3 + q^3 = (5 \times 5 \times 5) + ((-2) \times (-2) \times (-2))$ 　| work out each term first before you add |
$\qquad = 125 + (-8)$
$\qquad = 117$

d) $p^2 - 4qr = (5 \times 5) - (4 \times (-2) \times (-3))$
$\qquad\quad = 25 - (+24)$
$\qquad\quad = 1$

Here are some questions for you to try.

EXERCISE 18

1. Work out:
   a) $(-2) \times (-3) \times (-4)$ b) $(-1)^{10}$
   c) $(-4) \times (+5)^3$

2. Given that $s = -5$, $t = 4$ and $u = -6$, work out the value of:
   a) stu b) $(st)^3$
   c) $s^2 - u^2$ d) $s + tu$

Check your answers at the end of this module.

Division of directed numbers

The rules for signs in division are the same as those for multiplication. That is:

$$\text{(positive)} \div \text{(positive)} = \text{(positive)}$$
$$\text{(positive)} \div \text{(negative)} = \text{(negative)}$$
$$\text{(negative)} \div \text{(positive)} = \text{(negative)}$$
$$\text{(negative)} \div \text{(negative)} = \text{(positive)}$$

Examples and solutions

$(-20) \div (-4) = (+5)$ $(+56) \div (-7) = (-8)$
$(-12) \div (+8) = (-1.5)$ $(-6y) \div (2y) = (-3)$
$(-p^2) \div (-p) = (+p)$ $(8qr) \div (-2q) = (-4r)$

B Simplifying algebraic expressions

Removing brackets

In Unit 1 you learnt how to remove brackets from expressions such as $8(2a - 3b)$, $3(y - 2) + 2(3 - y)$ and $2g(g^2 + 3g - 4)$.

You will remember that, when a bracket is to be multiplied by a number or expression (written immediately in front of or behind the bracket), then *every* term inside the bracket is multiplied.

Thus $8(2a - 3b) = 16a - 24b$
     $3(y - 2) + 2(3 - y) = 3y - 6 + 6 - 2y = y$ [collecting like terms]
     $2g(g^2 + 3g - 4) = 2g^3 + 6g^2 - 8g$

You should note that $(2a - b)c$ is equal to $c(2a - b)$ so it is $2ac - bc$. This means that it makes no difference whether the multiplier is in front of or behind the bracket.

Do the following examples with me. This time you'll have to remember the rules for signs.

Example I

Remove the brackets and simplify:
a) $3(y + 7) - 2(4y - 5)$ b) $4(3s - 2t) - 3(s + 3t)$
c) $-5(6z - 1) + 6(2z - 3)$ d) $2(p + q) - (p - q)$

$(+) \times (+) = (+)$
$(-) \times (-) = (+)$
$(-) \times (+) = (-)$
$(+) \times (-) = (-)$

Solution

a) $3(y + 7) - 2(4y - 5)$
    $= 3y + 21 - 8y + 10$
    $= -5y + 31$

b) $4(3s - 2t) - 3(s + 3t)$
    $= 12s - 8t - 3s - 9t$
    $= 9s - 17t$

c) $-5(6z - 1) + 6(2z - 3)$
    $= -30z + 5 + 12z - 18$
    $= -18z - 13$

d) $2(p + q) - (p - q)$ $- (p - q)$ means $-1(p - q)$
    $= 2p + 2q - p + q$
    $= p + 3q.$

Example 2

Remove the brackets and simplify:
a) $2(e + 3f) - 3e + 4(e - f)$
b) $t(3t + 2) - (5t - 4) + 7$

Solution

a) $2(e + 3f) - 3e + 4(e - f)$
    $= 2e + 6f - 3e + 4e - 4f$
    $= 3e + 2f$

b) $t(3t + 2) - (5t - 4) + 7$
    $= 3t^2 + 2t - 5t + 4 + 7$
    $= 3t^2 - 3t + 11$

Here are some questions for you to do. Be careful with the signs!

EXERCISE 19

1. Remove the brackets and simplify:
    a) $4(y + 3) - 3(2y - 1)$ b) $2(3s - 4t) - 5(s + 2t)$
    c) $-3(2z - 1) + 7(3z - 2)$ d) $6(p + q) - (q - p)$

2. Remove the brackets and simplify:
    a) $3(2e + f) - 4f + 5(e - f)$ b) $t(2t + 1) - (4t - 3) - 5$

Check your answers at the end of this module.

Multiplying two brackets

You will sometimes have to remove the brackets from expressions of the form $(a + b)(c + d)$. This may be called 'expanding the brackets'. To explain how to do this I start with $(a + b)x = ax + bx$.
Do you agree? Now replace x by $(c + d)$.

So $(a + b)(c + d) = a(c + d) + b(c + d)$.

Now remove the remaining brackets:

$(a + b)(c + d) = ac + ad + bc + bd$

These examples will help you to get the idea:

Example 1

Remove the brackets and simplify:
a) $(p + q)(p + 2q)$ b) $(2s + 3t)(4s - 5t)$
c) $(t - 2)(t + 3)$

Solution

a) $(p + q)(p + 2q) = p(p + 2q) + q(p + 2q)$
$= p^2 + 2pq + qp + 2q^2$
$= p^2 + 3pq + 2q^2$ $\boxed{qp = pq}$

b) $(2s + 3t)(4s - 5t) = 2s(4s - 5t) + 3t(4s - 5t)$
$= 8s^2 - 10st + 12st - 15t^2$
$= 8s^2 + 2st - 15t^2$ $\boxed{ts = st}$

c) $(t - 2)(t + 3) = t(t + 3) - 2(t + 3)$
$= t^2 + 3t - 2t - 6$
$= t^2 + t - 6$

Example 2

Expand the brackets and simplify:
a) $(2y - 1)(3 - 4y)$ b) $(5p - 3)^2$
c) $(s - 3)(s^2 - s - 4)$

Solution

a) $(2y - 1)(3 - 4y) = 2y(3 - 4y) - 1(3 - 4y)$
$= 6y - 8y^2 - 3 + 4y$
$= -8y^2 + 10y - 3$

b) $(5p - 3)^2 = (5p - 3)(5p - 3)$
$= 5p(5p - 3) - 3(5p - 3)$
$= 25p^2 - 15p - 15p + 9$
$= 25p^2 - 30p + 9$

c) $(s - 3)(s^2 - s - 4) = s(s^2 - s - 4) - 3(s^2 - s - 4)$
$= s^3 - s^2 - 4s - 3s^2 + 3s + 12$
$= s^3 - 4s^2 - s + 12$

Some important expansions

There are three expansions of brackets which occur quite frequently and are worth remembering.

First, it is often useful to be able to find the square of two numbers added together.

$(a + b)^2 = (a + b)(a + b) = a(a + b) + b(a + b)$
$= a^2 + ab + ab + b^2$
$= a^2 + 2ab + b^2$ $\boxed{ba = ab}$

Secondly, you should also know how to find the square of the difference between two numbers.

$(a - b)^2 = (a - b)(a - b) = a(a - b) - b(a - b)$
$= a^2 - ab - ba + b^2$
$= a^2 - 2ab + b^2$ $\boxed{ba = ab}$

A third result which is often needed is the 'difference of two squares'.

$$(a - b)(a + b) = a(a + b) - b(a + b)$$
$$= a^2 + ab - ba - b^2$$
$$= a^2 - b^2$$

$$\boxed{ba = ab}$$

Here are the results you should try to remember:

$$(a + b)^2 = a^2 + 2ab + b^2$$
$$(a - b)^2 = a^2 - 2ab + b^2$$
$$(a - b)(a + b) = a^2 - b^2$$

Here is some practice for you on expanding brackets.

EXERCISE 20

1. Remove the brackets and simplify:
    a) $(t - 5)(t - 4)$ b) $(2p - 1)(3p + 1)$
    c) $(4s + 3t)(3s - 4t)$

2. Expand the brackets and simplify:
    a) $(3p + 2)^2$ b) $(4y - 3)(4y + 3)$
    c) $(s - 2)(s^2 + 2s - 3)$

Check your answers at the end of this module.

C Factorising algebraic expressions

Now that you've learnt how to remove brackets, I'm going to show you how to put them back again! It's called **factorising**.

> Factorising is just the reverse of removing brackets.

Consider what you do when you are asked to factorise a number, say 30. You try to find two or more numbers which, when multiplied together, give 30.

30 factorised could be 3×10 but there are alternatives such as 5×6, 2×15 and $2 \times 3 \times 5$. Usually you want the number to be factorised *completely* (sometimes we say 'as far as possible'). So if you factorised the number 30 completely you would have $30 = 2 \times 3 \times 5$.

In algebra, we have the same situation. For example, the factorised form of $18p$ is $2 \times 3 \times 3 \times p$ and the factorised form of $4q$ is $2 \times 2 \times q$.

Common factors

To factorise an expression such as $18p + 4q$, you look for something which is a factor of both $18p$ and $4q$.

Looking at $18p = 2 \times 3 \times 3 \times p$
       and $4q = 2 \times 2 \times q$
you can see that the only number they have in common is 2.
When you divide $18p$ by 2, you get $3 \times 3 \times p$, that is $9p$, and when you divide $4q$ by 2, you get $2 \times q$, that is $2q$.

Hence the factorised form of $18p + 4q$ is $2(9p + 2q)$.
The result can be checked by removing the brackets and you should do this whenever you have factorised an expression.

Example 1

Factorise:

a) $18s + 12t + 24u$ b) $9pq - 6qr$

c) $20yz - 5z$

Solution

a)   Factorising each term: $18s = 2 \times 3 \times 3 \times s$

$12t = 2 \times 2 \times 3 \times t$

$24u = 2 \times 2 \times 3 \times u$

These terms have 2×3 in common, that is 6

$18s \div 6 = 3s$, $12t \div 6 = 2t$ and $24u \div 6 = 4u$

so $18s + 12t + 24u = 6(3s + 2t + 4u)$ $\boxed{\text{check by removing the brackets}}$

b)   Factorising each term: $9pq = 3 \times 3 \times p \times q$

$6qr = 2 \times 3 \times q \times r$

These terms have $3 \times q$ in common, that is $3q$.

$9pq \div 3q = 3p$ and $6qr \div 3q = 2r$

so $9pq - 6qr = 3q(3p - 2r)$

c)   Factorising each term: $20yz = 2 \times 2 \times 5 \times y \times z$

$5z = 5 \times z$

These terms have $5 \times z$ in common, that is $5z$.

$20yz \div 5z = 4y$ and $5z \div 5z = 1$

so $20yz - 5z = 5z(4y - 1)$

Example 2

Factorise:

a) $t^2 - 2t$ b) $4y^2 - 6yz$

c) $12p^2q - 9pq^2 + 15pq$

Solution

a) $t^2 = t \times t$ and $2t = 2 \times t$. These have a factor t in common.

So $t^2 - 2t = t(t - 2)$.

b) $5y^2 = 2 \times 2 \times y \times y$ and $6yz = 2 \times 3 \times y \times z$.

These have $2 \times y$ in common.

So $4y^2 - 6yz = 2y(2y - 3z)$.

c) $12p^2q = 2 \times 2 \times 3 \times p \times p \times q$ These have

$9pq^2 = 3 \times 3 \times p \times q \times q$ $3 \times p \times q$

$15pq = 3 \times 5 \times p \times q$ in common.

So $12p^2q - 9pq^2 + 15pq = 3pq(4p - 3q + 5)$.

Try this exercise:

EXERCISE 21

1. Factorise:
   a) $10s + 15t + 20u$ b) $12pq - 9qr$
   c) $16yz - 4y$

2. Factorise:
   a) $t^2 + 5t$ b) $9y^2 - 6yz$
   c) $6p^2q + 14pq^2 - 10pq$

Check your answers at the end of this module.

CORE learners should now turn to the end of the unit for the 'Summary' and 'Check your progress'. The remainder of this unit covers the work on algebraic manipulation which is in the EXTENDED syllabus but not the CORE syllabus.

Factorising by grouping

Some expressions which have four terms (or any even number of terms) can be factorised by first grouping the terms in pairs and then using the 'common factor' method on each pair.

Here is a simple example: $ab + 2a + bc + 2c$
$$= a(b + 2) + c(b + 2)$$

The method will only succeed if the contents of the two brackets are *exactly* the same, so that the bracket forms the common factor at the next step.

In this example, both brackets are $(b + 2)$ so we can proceed
$a(b + 2) + c(b + 2) = (b + 2)(a + c)$.

This result can be checked by expanding the brackets.

It is worth remembering that $- a - b = - (a + b)$
             and $b - a = -(- b + a) = -(a - b)$.

In both of these examples I have *taken out* a '−' sign.

Example 1

Factorise $ap + aq - bp - bq$.

Solution

$$ap + aq - bp - bq = a(p + q) - b(p + q)$$
$$= (p + q)(a - b)$$

Example 2

Factorise $6b^2 + 4bd + 3bc + 2cd$.

Solution

$$6b^2 + 4bd + 3bc + 2cd = 2b(3b + 2d) + c(3b + 2d)$$
$$= (3b + 2d)(2b + c)$$

Example 3

Factorise $3t^2 - 2t - 15t + 10$.

Solution

$$\begin{aligned}
3\widehat{t^2 - 2t} - \widehat{15t + 10} &= t(3t - 2) - 5(3t - 2) \\
&= (3t - 2)(t - 5)
\end{aligned}$$

Example 4

Factorise $3y + 4pq - 3p - 4yq$.

Solution

Notice that pairing the first two terms and the last two terms will not enable us to do any factorisation. We try a different pairing by changing the order of the terms:

$$\begin{aligned}
3\widehat{y + 4pq} - \widehat{3p - 4yq} &= 3y - 3p + 4pq - 4yq \\
&= 3(y - p) + 4q(p - y)
\end{aligned}$$

The contents of the two brackets are not exactly the same. But remember that you can change $(p - y)$ by taking out a '$-$' so $(p - y) = -(y - p)$ and then we obtain:

$$\begin{aligned}
3y + 4pq - 3p - 4yq &= 3(y - p) - 4q(y - p) \\
&= (y - p)(3 - 4q)
\end{aligned}$$

Example 5

Factorise $6ab - 3bc + 2ad - cd + 8a - 4c$.

Solution

$$\begin{aligned}
6\widehat{ab - 3bc} &+ 2\widehat{ad - cd} + 8\widehat{a - 4c} \\
= 3b(2a - c) &+ d(2a - c) + 4(2a - c) \\
= (2a - c)&(3b + d + 4)
\end{aligned}$$

Factorising quadratic expressions

Removing the brackets from expressions such as $(2x - 3)(x + 4)$ is a matter of following rules:

$$\begin{aligned}
(2x - 3)(x + 4) &= 2x(x + 4) - 3(x + 4) \\
&= 2x^2 + 8x - 3x - 12 \\
&= 2x^2 + 5x - 12
\end{aligned}$$

Factorising an expression such as $2x^2 + 5x - 12$ is the reverse of removing brackets. However, factorising such expressions is more a matter of trial and error than following rules.

> *Trial and error* means there is no rule to find the answer. You must find the answer by testing different possibilities.

Expressions of the form $ax^2 + bx + c$ (where a, b and c are numbers) are called **quadratic expressions**. The difficulty in factorising such expressions is due to the fact that the term bx is, in fact, a combination of two terms.

In the example above, the $5x$ came from $+8x - 3x$.
When trying to factorise $2x^2 + 5x - 12$, how do you decide that $5x$ came from $+8x - 3x$ and not from $+7x - 2x$ or $11x - 6x$ or some other pair of terms?

I'll start with quadratic expressions which have a single x^2.
For example, $x^2 + 8x + 12$.

The factorised form of this expression must be $(x + a)(x + b)$, where a and b are numbers we have to find.

Now $(x + a)(x + b) = x(x + b) + a(x + b)$
$$= x^2 + bx + ax + ab$$
$$= x^2 + (a + b)x + ab$$

Can you see that the numbers a and b must satisfy $a + b = +8$ and $ab = +12$?

Now find a and b by trial and error.

It is best to start by expressing $+12$ as the product of two factors. I could have $(+1) \times (+12)$, $(+2) \times (+6)$, $(+3) \times (+4)$, $(-1) \times (-12)$, ... I must choose the two factors which add up to $+8$. These are $+2$ and $+6$.

Now I can factorise the expression as follows:
$$x^2 + 8x + 12 = x^2 + 2x + 6x + 12$$
$$= x(x + 2) + 6(x + 2)$$
$$= (x + 2)(x + 6)$$

> always check that you've found the right factors by multiplying the brackets

With practice you will be able to factorise these quadratic expressions without writing down the working. The numbers in the brackets are the factors of $+12$ which add up to $+8$.

Example 1

Factorise $x^2 + 2x - 15$.

Solution

I must find two numbers which when multiplied give -15
and when added give $+2$.

I start with -1 and $+15$; no good – these add up to $+14$.
-3 and $+5$; success! – these add up to $+2$.
$$x^2 + 2x - 15 = x^2 - 3x + 5x - 15$$
$$= x(x - 3) + 5(x - 3)$$
$$= (x - 3)(x + 5)$$

Example 2

Factorise $x^2 - 5x - 24$.

Solution

I must find two numbers which when multiplied give -24
and when added give -5.

I start with -24 and $+1$; no good – these add up to -23.
-12 and $+2$; no good – these add up to -10.
-3 and 8; no good – these add up to $+5$.
But that last pair was close. What if I change the signs?
$+3$ and -8; success – now they add up to -5.

$$x^2 - 5x - 24 = x^2 + 3x - 8x - 24$$
$$= x(x + 3) - 8(x + 3)$$
$$= (x + 3)(x - 8)$$

Factorising $ax^2 + bx + c$

When the coefficient of x^2 in the quadratic expression is not 1, the procedure for factorising the expression is similar to the one I described above. In this case, you need to find two numbers which when multiplied give ac and when added together give b. These two numbers indicate how the term bx in the expression has to be split up. You'll understand what I mean more easily by looking at the examples.

Example 1

Factorise $3x^2 + 2x - 8$.

Solution

I must find two numbers which when multiplied give $(3)(-8) = -24$ and when added give $+2$.

I start with -1 and $+24$; no good – these add up to $+23$.
$\qquad\qquad -2$ and $+12$; no good – these add up to $+10$.
$\qquad\qquad -3$ and $+8$; no good – these add up to $+5$.
$\qquad\qquad -4$ and $+6$; success! – these add up to $+2$.

$$3x^2 + 2x - 8 = 3x^2 - 4x + 6x - 8$$
$$= x(3x - 4) + 2(3x - 4)$$
$$= (3x - 4)(x + 2)$$

Example 2

Factorise $6x^2 - 7x + 2$.

Solution

I must find two numbers which when multiplied give $(6)(+2) = +12$ and when added give -7.

Think carefully. Can you see that to get factors of $+12$ both the numbers must be positive or both the numbers must be negative. But the numbers must add to -7. So both the numbers must be negative.

I start with -1 and -12; no good – these add up to -13.
$\qquad\qquad -2$ and -6; no good – these add up to -8.
$\qquad\qquad -3$ and -4; success! – these add up to -7.

$$6x^2 - 7x + 2 = 6x^2 - 3x - 4x + 2$$
$$= 3x(2x - 1) - 2(2x - 1)$$
$$= (2x - 1)(3x - 2)$$

Factorising a difference of two squares

Do you remember I showed you this:

$(a - b)(a + b) = a^2 - b^2$ which I said is called *the difference of two squares.*

This result is usually used the other way round – to factorise $a^2 - b^2$. For example, $9x^2 - 16y^2$ can be written as $(3x)^2 - (4y)^2$. It is, therefore, the difference between two squares.

In the above result, write $3x$ in place of a and $4y$ in place of b:

$$9x^2 - 16y^2 = (3x)^2 - (4y)^2$$
$$= (3x - 4y)(3x + 4y)$$

Here are two more examples:

$$t^2 - 25 = (t)^2 - (5)^2 = (t - 5)(t + 5)$$
$$64d^2 - 1 = (8d)^2 - (1)^2 = (8d - 1)(8d + 1)$$

This method may seem to be of no use in factorising some two term differences. For example, since 18 and 8 are not perfect squares, it seems that $18x^2 - 8$ cannot be factorised using the 'difference of two squares' method. However, if you see that 18 and 8 have a common factor, you can factorise the expression as follows:

$$18x^2 - 8 = 2[9x^2 - 4]$$
$$= 2[(3x)^2 - (2)^2]$$
$$= 2(3x - 2)(3x + 2)$$

Whenever you're trying to factorise any algebraic expression, you should first look to see if the terms have a common factor. After dealing with the common factor, you may find that you can complete the factorisation by using *difference of two squares* or the method of grouping or the method we have described for quadratic expressions. The result $a^2 - b^2 = (a - b)(a + b)$ can also be used to work out arithmetical expressions.

For example, in $(1234)^2 - (1230)^2$ you take 1234 as a and 1230 as b and you get $(1234)^2 - (1230)^2 = (1234 - 1230)(1234 + 1230)$

$$= (4)(2464)$$
$$= 9856$$

Similarly $(6\frac{1}{4})^2 - (3\frac{3}{4})^2 = (6\frac{1}{4} - 3\frac{3}{4})(6\frac{1}{4} + 3\frac{3}{4})$

$$= (2\frac{1}{2})(10)$$
$$= 25$$

It's quite a long time since you had the opportunity to test your understanding of the work. Here are some questions on factorisation for you to try.

EXERCISE 22

1. Factorise:
    a) $3y + 9z + by + 3bz$
    b) $4p + 6r - 2pq - 3qr$
    c) $3x^2 - 4x + 6x - 8$
    d) $ac - bc - ad + bd$

2. Factorise:
    a) $x^2 + 14x + 24$
    b) $x^2 + x - 6$
    c) $x^2 - 8x + 15$

3. Factorise:
   a) $3x^2 + 11x + 6$ b) $5x^2 - 9x - 2$
   c) $4x^2 - 8x + 3$

4. Work out:
   a) $(10\ 001)^2 - (10\ 000)^2$ b) $(51)^2 - (49)^2$
   c) $(6\frac{1}{4})^2 - (5\frac{3}{4})^2$

5. Factorise:
   a) $4x^2 - 9y^2$ b) $36a^2 - 25b^2$
   c) $16c^2 - 1$ d) $27x^2 - 12y^2$

Check your answers at the end of this module.

Manipulating algebraic fractions

Algebraic fractions can be simplified, added, subtracted, multiplied and divided in the same way as fractions in arithmetic. Finding the factors of the numerator and denominator of a fraction plays an important part in all these processes.

You will often need to make use of the fact that, if you multiply the numerator and denominator of a fraction by the same number or algebraic expression, the value of the fraction does not change. Similarly, if you divide the numerator and denominator of a fraction by the same number or algebraic expression, the value of the fraction does not change.

Example 1

Simplify:

a) $\dfrac{6pq}{8p^2}$ b) $\dfrac{y^2 + 5y}{y^2 + 6y + 5}$

c) $\dfrac{x^2 - 4}{x^2 - 5x + 6}$

Solution

> Dividing the numerator and denominator of a fraction by the same number is often called *cancelling*.

a) $6pq = 2 \times 3 \times p \times q$ and $8p^2 = 2 \times 2 \times 2 \times p \times p$.

These expressions have $2 \times p$ in common so you can divide the numerator and denominator of the fraction by $2p$.

$\dfrac{6pq}{8p^2} = \dfrac{6pq \div 2p}{8p^2 \div 2p} = \dfrac{3q}{4p}$

b) Using the 'common factor' method, $y^2 + 5y = y(y + 5)$.
Using the 'quadratic expression' method,
$y^2 + 6y + 5 = (y + 1)(y + 5)$.
These expressions have $(y + 5)$ in common so you can *cancel* this factor from the numerator and denominator.

So $\dfrac{y^2 + 5y}{y^2 + 6y + 5} = \dfrac{y\cancel{(y + 5)}}{(y + 1)\cancel{(y + 5)}} = \dfrac{y}{y + 1}$

Note: 'Cancelling' means 'cancelling a *factor* which is common to the numerator and denominator'. You must not, for example, think that you can cancel the y^2 which appears in the numerator and denominator of the given fraction. This would be a *subtraction* from the numerator and denominator and this would change the value of the fraction.

c)   Using the 'difference of squares', $x^2 - 4 = (x - 2)(x + 2)$.
     Using the 'quadratic expression' method,
     $x^2 - 5x + 6 = (x - 2)(x - 3)$

     So $\dfrac{x^2 - 4}{x^2 - 5x + 6} = \dfrac{(x - 2)(x + 2)}{(x - 2)(x - 3)} = \dfrac{(x + 2)}{(x - 3)}$

Example 2

Express as a single fraction in its simplest form:

a) $\dfrac{12yz}{5} \times \dfrac{10y}{9z}$ b) $\dfrac{x^2 + 2x - 3}{x^2 + 3x} \times \dfrac{3x}{x^2 - 1}$

c) $\dfrac{p^2 + 2p}{p - 4} \div \dfrac{p^2 - 4}{2p - 8}$

Solution

a)   The numerator and denominator have 5, 3 and z in common so
     these factors can be cancelled. (That means you divide the
     numerator and denominator by each of these factors.)

     $\dfrac{12yz}{5} \times \dfrac{10y}{9z} = \dfrac{\overset{4}{12yz}}{\underset{1}{5}} \times \dfrac{\overset{2}{10y}}{\underset{3}{9z}} = \dfrac{4y}{1} \times \dfrac{2y}{3} = \dfrac{8y^2}{3}$

b) $\dfrac{x^2 + 2x - 3}{x^2 + 3x} \times \dfrac{3x}{x^2 - 1} = \dfrac{(x - 1)(x + 3)}{x(x + 3)} \times \dfrac{3x}{(x - 1)(x + 1)}$

     $= \dfrac{3}{x + 1}$

c)   Dividing by a number or an expression is equivalent to
     multiplying by its reciprocal, so

     $\dfrac{p^2 + 2p}{p - 4} \div \dfrac{p^2 - 4}{2p - 8} = \dfrac{p^2 + 2p}{p - 4} \times \dfrac{2p - 8}{p^2 - 4}$

     $= \dfrac{p(p + 2)}{(p - 4)} \times \dfrac{2(p - 4)}{(p - 2)(p + 2)}$

     $= \dfrac{2p}{(p - 2)}$

Example 3

Express as a single fraction in its simplest form:

a) $\dfrac{3d}{4} + \dfrac{9d}{10}$ b) $\dfrac{t}{3} - \dfrac{t - 4}{2}$ c) $\dfrac{1}{x - 2} - \dfrac{2}{x - 3}$

Solution

Fractions can be added and subtracted only when they have the
same denominator. Since the final answer is required in its simplest
form, this common denominator should be the simplest (or lowest)
possible.

a)   20 is the lowest number which is a multiple of 4 and a multiple
     of 10.

     $\dfrac{3d}{4} = \dfrac{15d}{20}$ multiplying numerator and denominator by 5

     and $\dfrac{9d}{10} = \dfrac{18d}{20}$ multiplying numerator and denominator by 2

     so $\dfrac{3d}{4} + \dfrac{9d}{10} = \dfrac{15d}{20} + \dfrac{18d}{20} = \dfrac{33d}{20}$

b)   6 is the lowest common multiple of 3 and 2.

$\dfrac{t}{3} = \dfrac{2t}{6}$ and $\dfrac{t-4}{2} = \dfrac{3(t-4)}{6}$ the brackets are essential!

so $\dfrac{t}{3} - \dfrac{t-4}{2} = \dfrac{2t}{6} - \dfrac{3(t-4)}{6} = \dfrac{2t - 3(t-4)}{6}$

$= \dfrac{2t - 3t + 12}{6}$ be careful with the signs!

$= \dfrac{12 - t}{6}$

c)   Neither $x - 2$ nor $x - 3$ can be factorised so the simplest expression which is a multiple of each of them is $(x - 2)(x - 3)$.

$\dfrac{1}{x-2} = \dfrac{(x-3)}{(x-2)(x-3)}$ multiply numerator and denominator by $(x - 3)$

and $\dfrac{2}{x-3} = \dfrac{2(x-2)}{(x-3)(x-2)}$ multiply numerator and denominator by $(x - 2)$

so $\dfrac{1}{x-2} - \dfrac{2}{x-3} = \dfrac{(x-3)}{(x-2)(x-3)} - \dfrac{2(x-2)}{(x-3)(x-2)}$

$= \dfrac{(x-3) - 2(x-2)}{(x-2)(x-3)}$

$= \dfrac{x - 3 - 2x + 4}{(x-2)(x-3)}$

$= \dfrac{1-x}{(x-2)(x-3)}$ it is usual to leave the denominator in factorised form

Example 4

Simplify: $\dfrac{3x+4}{x^2 + x - 6} - \dfrac{1}{x+3}$

Solution

$\dfrac{3x+4}{x^2 + x - 6} - \dfrac{1}{x+3}$

$= \dfrac{3x+4}{(x+3)(x-2)} - \dfrac{1}{(x+3)}$

$= \dfrac{3x+4}{(x+3)(x-2)} - \dfrac{(x-2)}{(x+3)(x-2)}$ LCM of denominator is $(x + 3)(x - 2)$

$= \dfrac{3x+4 - (x-2)}{(x+3)(x-2)}$

$= \dfrac{3x+4 - x + 2}{(x+3)(x-2)}$

$= \dfrac{2x+6}{(x+3)(x-2)}$ factorise the numerator

$= \dfrac{2(x+3)}{(x+3)(x-2)}$

$= \dfrac{2}{(x-2)}$

You have now seen how factorisation can help you when you are manipulating algebraic fractions. Apply your knowledge to the following questions.

EXERCISE 23

1. Simplify:

   a) $\dfrac{4p^2q}{6pq^2}$

   b) $\dfrac{y^2 + 3y}{y^2 + 8y + 15}$

   c) $\dfrac{x^2 - 2x}{x^2 - 7x + 10}$

2. Express as a single fraction in its simplest form:

   a) $\dfrac{3a}{4b} \times \dfrac{5ab}{3}$

   b) $\dfrac{x^2}{x^2 - 4} \times \dfrac{x^2 + 3x + 2}{2x}$

   c) $\dfrac{3p - 6}{p^2 - p - 6} \div \dfrac{p - 2}{p + 2}$

3. Express as a single fraction in its simplest form:

   a) $\dfrac{3a}{4} - \dfrac{7a}{10}$

   b) $\dfrac{2x}{3} - \dfrac{3(x - 5)}{2}$

   c) $\dfrac{2}{t + 1} + \dfrac{3}{t + 2}$

4. Simplify: $\dfrac{2(x + 2)}{x^2 + 4x - 5} - \dfrac{1}{x + 5}$

Check your answers at the end of this module.

D   Transforming more complicated formulae

In Unit 1 Section C you learnt how to change the subject of simple formulae. Now you know how to remove brackets, how to factorise algebraic expressions and how to manipulate algebraic fractions, you will be able to deal with more complicated formulae.

The methods you use for more complicated formulae are the same as for simple formulae, but usually you will have to do more manipulation and you will need to be more careful, particularly in handling the signs and the brackets.

You must remember that when you handle a formula, you can:
- add the same quantity to both sides
- subtract the same quantity from both sides
- multiply both sides by the same quantity
- divide both sides by the same non-zero quantity
- square or cube both sides or, generally, take the same power of both sides
- take the square root or the cube root of both sides or, generally, take the nth root of both sides.

The steps you usually take in manipulating a formula include the following:
- clear the formula of any fractions (by multiplying both sides by an appropriate number or expression)
- eliminate any square root or other root (by squaring or cubing or . . .)
- expand any brackets

- rearrange the terms so that those containing the new subject are isolated on one side of the formula (by adding quantities to both sides or subtracting quantities from both sides)
- factorise this side so it is (new subject) × (expression)
- divide both sides by (expression) so formula becomes (new subject) = . . .

Here are some examples of the methods we use.

Example 1

Given that $ab + c = d(b + 2)$, express b in terms of a, c and d.

> this means 'make b the subject of the formula'

Solution

$$ab + c = d(b + 2)$$ ⟶ expand the brackets

$$ab + c = db + 2d$$ ⟶ collect terms containing b on one side

$$ab - db = 2d - c$$ ⟶ factorise as b × (expression)

$$b(a - d) = 2d - c$$ ⟶ divide by both sides by (expression)

$$b = \frac{2d - c}{(a - d)}$$

Example 2

Make u the subject of the formula $\frac{1}{v} + \frac{1}{u} = \frac{2}{R}$.

Solution

$$\frac{vuR}{v} + \frac{vuR}{u} = \frac{2vuR}{R}$$ ⟶ multiply by vuR (to clear the fractions)

$$uR + vR = 2vu$$ ⟶ collect terms containing u on one side

$$vR = 2vu - uR$$ ⟶ factorise as u × (expression)

$$vR = u(2v - R)$$ ⟶ divide both sides by (expression)

$$\frac{vR}{(2v - R)} = u$$

The required formula is $u = \frac{vR}{(2v - R)}$.

Example 3

Make b the subject of the formula $r = \frac{a - b}{a + b}$.

Solution

$$r(a + b) = a - b$$ ⟶ multiply both sides by $a + b$ (to clear the fraction)

$$ra + rb = a - b$$ ⟶ expand the bracket

$$rb + b = a - ra$$ ⟶ collect terms containing b on one side

$$b(r + 1) = a - ra$$ ⟶ factorise as b × (expression)

$$b = \frac{a - ra}{(r + 1)}$$ ⟶ divide both sides by (expression)

This could be written as $b = \frac{a(1 - r)}{(1 + r)}$.

Example 4

Given that $F = \dfrac{R}{R+r}$, express R in terms of F and r.

Solution

$F(R + r) = R$ multiply both sides by $R + r$ (to clear the fraction)

$FR + Fr = R$ expand the bracket

$Fr = R - FR$ collect terms containing R on one side

$Fr = R(1 - F)$ factorise as $R \times$ (expression)

$\dfrac{Fr}{(1 - F)} = R$ divide both sides by (expression)

The required formula is $R = \dfrac{Fr}{(1 - F)}$.

Example 5

Make a the subject of the formula $T = 2\pi\sqrt{\dfrac{a}{g}}$.

Solution

Divide both sides by 2π to isolate the square root

$\dfrac{T}{2\pi} = \sqrt{\dfrac{a}{g}}$

$\dfrac{T^2}{4\pi^2} = \dfrac{a}{g}$ square both sides

$\dfrac{gT^2}{4\pi^2} = a$ multiply both sides by g

The required formula is $a = \dfrac{gT^2}{4\pi^2}$.

Here are some for you to try.

EXERCISE 24

1. Given that $p(x + q) = x + r$, express x in terms of p, q and r.

2. Make y the subject of the formula $\dfrac{x}{a} + \dfrac{y}{b} = 1$.

3. Change the subject of the formula $y = \dfrac{x+3}{x-2}$ to x.

4. Make f the subject of the formula $s = ut + \frac{1}{2}ft^2$.

5. Given that $p = 3\sqrt{q} - 4$, express q in terms of p.

Check your answers at the end of this module.

Summary

This unit began with a section reminding you about how to add and subtract directed numbers – remember to use a number line to help you. The rules for multiplying directed numbers are:

- '+' $\times$ '+' = '+'
- '–' $\times$ '–' = '+'
- '+' $\times$ '–' = '–'
- '–' $\times$ '+' = '–'

The rules for signs when you are dividing are the same as the rules for multiplying.

You used these rules when you simplified algebraic expressions by removing brackets and collecting *like* terms.

Remember that when you multiply brackets you must multiply everything in the one bracket with everything in the other bracket. It's also worth remembering the following special cases:

- $(a + b)^2 = a^2 + 2ab + b^2$
- $(a - b)^2 = a^2 - 2ab + b^2$
- $(a - b)(a + b) = a^2 - b^2$ [difference of two squares]

You learnt how to factorise by:

- taking out a common factor
- grouping
- factorising quadratic expressions
- factorising the difference of two squares.

Factorising is useful for simplifying algebraic fractions:

- factorise the numerator and denominator if possible and then cancel.

You should now feel confident about the basics of working with algebraic expressions. You'll need to have these skills for solving equations and inequalities in the final unit of this module.

Check your progress

1. Rearrange the following expressions in numerical order, putting the smallest one first:

   $(-2)^4$, $2(-5)^2$, $(-0.9)^3$, $(-3)^2 - 4(+2)(-6)$, $(+9) \div (-\frac{1}{3})$

2. a) Find the value of $2t^2 - 3t - 1$ when $t = -4$.
   b) Find the value of $(t - 3)(2t + 1)$ when $t = -2$.

3. a) Expand $2y(y^2 - 3y - 5)$.
   b) Expand $(s - 4t) - (3s - 2t)$ and factorise your answer.

4. a) Factorise $15a - 9b + 12$.
   b) Factorise completely $9x^2y - 12xy^2 + 15xy$.

5. a) Find the product of $(x + 3)$ and $(3x - 2)$ expressing your answer in its simplest form.
   b) Factorise $2t^2 - 3t - 2$.

6. a) Express $\frac{2}{v} - \frac{1}{v + 1}$ as a single fraction in its simplest form.
   b) Given that $V = \frac{1}{3}\pi r^2 h + \frac{2}{3}\pi r^3$, find a formula for h in terms of π, r and V.
   Give your answer as a single fraction, in its simplest form.

Check your answers at the end of this module.

Unit 4
Solving Equations and Inequalities

In Unit 1 Section B you learnt how to solve equations such as $3x - 8 = 39$, $3n - 7 = n + 5$ and $2(x - 4) = 18$. Each of these equations contains just one unknown and 'solve the equation' means that you have to find the value of the unknown. Often, problems involve not just one unknown, but two or even more. In this section you will learn how to solve some problems which involve two unknowns.

This unit is divided into three sections:

Section	Title	Time
A	Solving simultaneous equations	3 hours
B	Solving quadratic equations	4 hours
C	Solving simple linear inequalities	3 hours

By the end of this unit, you should be able to:

- solve simultaneous linear equations
- solve quadratic equations
- solve simple linear inequalities.

A Solving simultaneous equations

Consider the following situation:

In a café, Jan is charged R11 for a bun and two cups of coffee. How much does a bun cost and how much does a cup of coffee cost? If you let b rand be the cost of a bun and c rand be the cost of a cup of coffee, you can write the equation $b + 2c = 11$.

This equation has two unknowns and there are many pairs of values of b an c which satisfy it. For example, $b = 5$ and $c = 3$ satisfy the equation. So do $b = 6$ and $c = 2.50$, and so do $b = 3$ and $c = 4$. You don't have enough information to answer the question.

Suppose now you are told that, in the same café, Nosipho was charged R10 for two buns and one cup of coffee.

You can write the equation $2b + c = 10$. Taking this equation on its own, you can find many pairs of values of b and c which satisfy it. For example, $b = 2$ and $c = 6$, or $b = 3.50$ and $c = 3$, or $b = 3$ and $c = 4$.

When you consider the equations $b + 2c = 11$ and $2b + c = 10$ *together*, there is only one pair of values which satisfies both of them: $b = 3$ and $c = 4$. Check (by substituting) to make sure that you agree that $b = 3$ and $c = 4$ make *both* equations true. You can now answer the original question – a bun costs R3 and a cup of coffee costs R4.

There are several methods (besides guessing) for solving equations such as $b + 2c = 11$, $2b + c = 10$. These equations are called **simultaneous equations** because you must find values of b and c which satisfy the two equations *at the same time* (simultaneously).

Substitution method

With this method you manipulate one equation to express one of the unknowns in terms of the other and then substitute this expression in the second equation. The method will become clear to you as you read through the following examples.

Example 1

Solve the simultaneous equations: $b + 2c = 11$
$$2b + c = 10.$$

Solution

First write the equations one below the other and call them ① and ②.
$$b + 2c = 11 \ldots ①$$
$$2b + c = 10 \ldots ②$$

From equation ①, we can see that: $\qquad b = 11 - 2c \ldots ③$

Substitute equation ③ into equation ②:

> wherever you see a b in equation ② you write $(11-2c)$ in its place

$$2(11 - 2c) + c = 10$$
$$22 - 4c + c = 10$$
$$-3c = 10 - 22$$
$$-3c = -12$$
$$c = (-12) \div (-3)$$
$$c = 4$$

Substitute this value of c into equation ③:
$$b = 11 - 8$$
$$b = 3$$

The solution of the simultaneous equations is $b = 3$ and $c = 4$. This solution should be checked by substitution in the original equations.

For ①, $b + 2c = 3 + 8 = 11$ ✓ $\quad\Big\}\quad$ The answer
For ②, $2b + c = 6 + 4 = 10$ ✓ $\qquad$ is checked.

Example 2

Solve the simultaneous equations: $x - 3y = 13$
$$3x + 2y = 6.$$

Solution

The equations are: $\qquad\qquad\qquad x - 3y = 13 \ldots ①$
$$3x + 2y = 6 \ldots ②$$

From equation ①: $\qquad\qquad\qquad x = 13 + 3y \ldots ③$

Substitute equation ③ into equation ②:
$$3(13 + 3y) + 2y = 6$$
$$39 + 9y + 2y = 6$$
$$11y = 6 - 39$$
$$11y = -33$$
$$y = -3$$

Substitute this value of y into equation ③:
$$x = 13 + (-9)$$
$$x = 4$$

The solution of the simultaneous equations is $x = 4$, $y = -3$.

Check: For equation ①: $x - 3y = 4 - 3(-3)$
$$= 4 + 9 = 13 \checkmark$$
For equation ②: $3x + 2y = 12 + 2(-3)$
$$= 12 - 6 = 6 \checkmark$$

$\left.\begin{array}{c}\\ \\ \\ \end{array}\right\}$ The answer is checked.

Example 3

In a canteen, 3 doughnuts and 2 hamburgers cost R6.50, and 1 doughnut and 3 hamburgers cost R6.25.

Find the cost of 1 doughnut and the cost of 1 hamburger.

Solution

Let d rand be the cost of 1 doughnut and h rand be the cost of 1 hamburger.

From the given information:
$$3d + 2h = 6.50 \ldots ①$$
$$d + 3h = 6.25 \ldots ②$$
From equation ②:
$$d = 6.25 - 3h \ldots ③$$

Substitute equation ③ into equation ①:
$$3(6.25 - 3h) + 2h = 6.50$$
$$18.75 - 9h + 2h = 6.50$$
$$-7h = 6.50 - 18.75$$
$$-7h = -12.25$$
$$h = 1.75$$

Substitute this value of h into equation ③:
$$d = 6.25 - 5.25$$
$$d = 1$$

1 doughnut costs R1 and 1 hamburger costs R1.75.

Check: Cost of 3 doughnuts and 2 hamburgers = R3 + R3.50 = R6.50 $\checkmark$
Cost of 1 doughnut and 3 hamburgers = R1 + R5.25 = R6.25 $\checkmark$

Method of equal coefficients

The method of substitution which I have just shown you is easy to use when the coefficient of one of the unknowns in one (or both) of the equations is 1 or -1. When none of the coefficients is 1 or -1, the method will involve fractions and it is easier to use the alternative **method of equal coefficients**. In this method, the coefficients of one of the unknowns in the two equations are made numerically equal, and then this unknown is eliminated by adding or subtracting the two equations.

This may sound complicated but it should become clear when you study the following examples.

Example 1

Solve the simultaneous equations: $3x + 2y = 12$
$5x - 3y = 1.$

Solution

Label the equations: $3x + 2y = 12 \ldots$ ①
$5x - 3y = 1 \ \ldots$ ②

You can make the coefficients of y numerically equal by multiplying both sides of equation ① by 3 and both sides of equation ② by 2.

Multiply equation ① by 3: $9x + 6y = 36 \ldots$ ③
Multiply equation ② by 2: $10x - 6y = 2 \ldots$ ④

The unknown y can now be eliminated by adding equations ③ and ④:

$$\begin{array}{r} 9x + 6y = 36 \\ \underline{10x - 6y = \ 2} \\ 19x \quad\quad = 38 \\ \text{so } x \quad\quad = 2 \end{array}$$

Substitute this value of x into equation ①: $6 + 2y = 12$
$2y = 6$
$y = 3$

The solution of the simultaneous equations is $x = 2$, $y = 3$.

Check: In equation ①: $3x + 2y = 6 + 6 = 12$ ✓ ⎱ The answer
In equation ②: $5x - 3y = 10 - 9 = 1$ ✓ ⎰ is checked.

Got the idea? I started by making the y's equal. I didn't have to. I could have made the x's equal by multiplying ① by 5 and ② by 3. Then I would have had to subtract ④ from equation ③ to get rid of the x term. Why don't you try it this way to check that you would get the same answer. *Remember when you subtract to change the signs.*

Example 2

Solve the simultaneous equations: $5u + 3y = 1$
$2u + 3v = -5.$

Solution

Label the equations: $5u + 3v = 1 \ldots$ ①
$2u + 3v = -5 \ldots$ ②

The coefficients of v in the two equations are already equal so you can eliminate v by subtracting equation ② from equation ①:

$$\begin{array}{r} 5u + 3v \ = 1 \\ \ominus \quad \ominus \quad\quad \oplus \\ \underline{2u + 3v \ = -5} \\ 3u \quad\quad = 6 \end{array}$$

remember to change the signs when you subtract

so $u = 2$

Substitute this value of u in equation ①:

$$10 + 3v = 1$$
$$3v = -9$$
$$v = -3$$

The solution of the simultaneous equations is $u = 2$, $v = -3$.

Check: In equation ①: $5u + 3v = 10 - 9 = 1$ ✓ $\Big\}$ The answer
In equation ②: $2u + 3v = 4 - 9 = -5$ ✓ is checked.

Example 3

Solve the simultaneous equations: $4x = y + 7$
$3x + 4y + 9 = 0$.

Solution

Re-arrange both equations and label them:

$$4x - y = 7 \quad \dots ①$$
$$3x + 4y = -9 \quad \dots ②$$

Multiply equation ① by 4: $16x - 4y = 28 \dots ③$
No change needed in equation ②: $\underline{3x + 4y = -9 \dots ④}$
Add equation ③ to equation ④: $19x = 19$
so $x = 1$

Substitute this value of x in equation ①: $4 - y = 7$
$-y = 3$
$y = -3$

The solution of the simultaneous equations is $x = 1$, $y = -3$.

Check: In equation ①: $4x = 4$ and
$y + 7 = -3 + 7 = 4$ ✓ $\left.\begin{array}{c} \\ \\ \\ \end{array}\right\}$ The answer
In equation ②: $3x + 4y + 9$ is checked.
$= 3 - 12 + 9 = 0$ ✓

Example 4

The variables x and y are related by $y = ax^2 + b$, where a and b are constants. It is given that $y = 11$ when $x = 2$ and that $y = 21$ when $x = 3$. Find the value of y when $x = 4$.

Solution

$$y = ax^2 + b$$
Using $y = 11$ when $x = 2$: $11 = 4a + b \dots ①$
Using $y = 21$ when $x = 3$: $21 = 9a + b \dots ②$

① and ② are simultaneous equations for the values of a and b.

Subtract equation ① from equation ②:
$$21 = 9a + b$$
$$\ominus \quad \ominus \quad \ominus$$
$$\underline{11 = 4a + b}$$
$$10 = 5a$$
$$\text{so } 2 = a$$

Substitute $a = 2$ in equation ①: $11 = 8 + b$

$3 = b$

Hence, the relationship between x and y is $y = 2x^2 + 3$.

When $x = 4$, $y = 2(16) + 3 = 32 + 3 = 35$.

Note: Since the coefficients of b in equations ① and ② are 1, the equations could also have been solved easily by the substitution method.

You should now be in a position to deal with the following problems. In each case you must decide whether to use the method of substitution to solve the simultaneous equations or to use the method of equal coefficients. Some of these questions can be done easily by either method.

EXERCISE 25

1. Solve the simultaneous equations:
    a) $3x + 2y = 10$ $4x - y = 6$
    b) $p + 2q = 7$ $3p - 2q = -3$
    c) $2u + v = 7$ $3u - 2v = 7$

2. Solve the simultaneous equations:
    a) $4s = 5t + 5$, $2s = 3t + 2$
    b) $6f - 6g = 5$, $3f - 4g = 1$
    c) $2x = 3y + 14$, $3x + 2y + 5 = 0$

3. Three notebooks and five pencils cost R10.
    One notebook and ten pencils cost R10.
    Taking the cost of a notebook to be n rand and the cost of a pencil to be p rand, write down two simultaneous equations. Solve the equations and state the cost of a notebook and the cost of a pencil.

4. The variables x and y are related by $y = mx + c$, where m and c are constants. It is given that $y = 12$ when $x = 2$ and that $y = 4$ when $x = 6$. Find the value of m and the value of c.

Did you remember to do a check on your answers? If so, you shouldn't need to be told how many you had right!

Check your answers at the end of this module.

If you are following the CORE syllabus, you should now turn to the end of the unit to the 'Summary' and the 'Check your progress'. The remainder of this unit covers work which is in the EXTENDED syllabus but not in the CORE syllabus.

?

B Solving quadratic equations

I'm thinking of a number.
When I multiply the number by itself, the answer is 144.
What number am I thinking of?

If your answer to this question is 12, then you are wrong!
The number I am thinking of is -12.

Solving this puzzle is equivalent to solving the equation $n^2 = 144$.
This equation has *two* solutions: $n = 12$ or $n = -12$.

So far (in Unit 1 Section B and Unit 4 Section A) you have met
equations which have only one solution. You are now going to deal
with quadratic equations, which usually have two solutions.

A **quadratic equation** is one which can be written in the form
$ax^2 + bx + c = 0$ where a, b and c are numbers and x is the unknown
whose value is to be found. (The equation *must* contain x^2 so the
number a must not be 0.)

You will remember that, in Unit 3, you learnt how to factorise a
quadratic expression. This will give you one method of solving
quadratic equations.

*Solving quadratic
equations by factors*

This method depends on a special property of the number 0, a
property that no other number has:

> If two numbers multiplied together give 0, then one
> of the numbers *must* be 0.

You *cannot* say:
'If two numbers multiplied together give 12, one of the numbers
must be 12'. You cannot say it because the number could be 2 and 6,
or 3 and 4, and there are many other possibilities.

So, 12 does not have the special property, nor does any number other
than 0.

The 'two numbers multiplied together' will be in the form of
algebraic expressions when you are solving equations. The following
examples will make the method clear.

Example 1

Solve the equation $x^2 - 5x = 0$.

Solution

Factorise the left-hand side using the 'common factor' method.
$$x(x - 5) = 0$$

Now there are two numbers x and $(x - 5)$ which are multiplied
together to give 0.

So $x = 0$ or $(x - 5) = 0$
$x = 0$ or $x = 5$

Example 2

Solve the equation $y^2 + 2y - 15 = 0$.

Solution

Factorise the left-hand side using the 'quadratic expression' method.
$$(y - 3)(y + 5) = 0$$

The two numbers $(y - 3)$ and $(y + 5)$ multiplied together give 0.
$$\text{So } (y - 3) = 0 \text{ or } (y + 5) = 0$$
$$y = 3 \text{ or } y = -5$$

Check: When $y = 3$, $y^2 + 2y - 15$
$$= 9 + 6 - 15 = 0 \checkmark$$
When $y = -5$, $y^2 + 2y - 15$
$$= 25 - 10 - 15 = 0 \checkmark$$
The answer is checked.

Example 3

Solve the equation $2x^2 - x = 6$.

Solution

The equation *must* be rearranged so that 0 appears at one side.
$$2x^2 - x - 6 = 0$$

To factorise the left-hand side, you need two numbers which when multiplied give $2(-6) = -12$, and when added give -1. These numbers are $+3$ and -4.

The equation is $2x^2 + 3x - 4x - 6 = 0$
$$x(2x + 3) - 2(2x + 3) = 0$$
$$(2x + 3)(x - 2) = 0$$
$$\text{so } (2x + 3) = 0 \text{ or } (x - 2) = 0$$
$$2x = -3 \text{ or } x = 2$$
$$x = -\tfrac{3}{2}x = -1.5 \text{ or } x = 2$$

Check: When $x = -1.5$, $2x^2 - x = 2(+2.25) - (-1.5) = 4.5 + 1.5 = 6 \checkmark$
When $x = 2$, $2x^2 - x = 2(4) - 2 = 8 - 2 = 6 \checkmark$

Example 4

Solve the equation $t(t + 3) = 40$.

Solution

The fact that the left-hand side is factorised does not help us because the right-hand side is 40. (The factorisation *would* have been helpful if the right-hand side had been 0.)

You must expand the brackets and rearrange:
$$t^2 + 3t = 40$$
$$t^2 + 3t - 40 = 0$$
$$(t + 8)(t - 5) = 0$$
$$\text{so } (t + 8) = 0 \text{ or } (t - 5) = 0$$
$$t = -8 \text{ or } t = 5 \quad \text{(Check this for yourself.)}$$

Example 5

Solve the equation $x^2 - 6x + 9 = 0$.

Solution

Factorising the left-hand side by the 'quadratic expression' method (or using $x^2 - 2ax + a^2 = (x - a)^2$ with $a = 3$):
$$(x - 3)(x - 3) = 0$$
$$\text{so } (x - 3) = 0 \text{ or } (x - 3) = 0$$
$$x = 3 \text{ or } x = 3$$

The solution of the quadratic equation is $x = 3$.

You will notice that there is only one value of x which satisfies this quadratic equation because the two factors happen to be exactly the same.

Example 6

Solve the equation $25t^2 - 16 = 0$.

Solution

The left-hand side is factorised by the 'difference of two squares' method:
$$(5t)^2 - (4)^2 = 0$$
$$(5t - 4)(5t + 4) = 0$$
$$\text{so } (5t - 4) = 0 \text{ or } (5t + 4) = 0$$
$$t = \frac{4}{5} \text{ or } t = -\frac{4}{5}$$

Example 7

20 years from now, a girl's age in years will be the square of her present age. Calculate her present age.

Solution

Let the girl's present age be n years.
20 years from now, her age will be $(n + 20)$ years.
Using the given information: $(n + 20) = n^2$
Rearranging to get 0 on one side: $0 = n^2 - n - 20$
Factorising the right-hand side: $0 = (n - 5)(n + 4)$
$$\text{so } (n - 5) = 0 \text{ or } (n + 4) = 0$$
$$n = 5 \text{ or } n = -4$$

Although the quadratic equation $(n + 20) = n^2$ has two solutions, one of them does not make sense. The girl cannot be -4 years old!

There is only one solution to the problem: the girl is 5 years old.

Check: In 20 years' time she will be 25 years old and $25 = 5^2$.

EXERCISE 26

1. Solve the quadratic equations:
   a) $x^2 + 7x = 0$
   b) $y^2 - 16 = 0$
   c) $(2t - 5)(t + 3) = 0$

2. Solve the quadratic equations:
   a) $x^2 - 7x + 12 = 0$
   b) $p^2 - 5p - 6 = 0$
   c) $n^2 + 8n + 16 = 0$

3. Solve the quadratic equations:
   a) $x^2 + 36 = 13x$
   b) $2y^2 = 3y + 2$
   c) $t(t + 4) = 12$

4. The square of a boy's present age in years is equal to 9 times his age 2 years ago. Calculate his present age.

Check your answers at the end of this module.

Solving quadratic equations by completing the square

You will find it difficult to factorise some quadratic expressions, and some you will not be able to factorise at all by the usual methods. For example, you will find it difficult to factorise $144x^2 - 17x - 36$ and you will not be able to factorise $x^2 - 3x + 1$ by the usual methods. Although the method of factors is the easiest way of solving many quadratic equations, you need another method for dealing with the more awkward cases.

One method is called **completing the square** and it makes use of a result you have already met: $x^2 + 2ax + a^2 = (x + a)^2$.

Consider the equation $n^2 = 144$.
We have already discovered that the solution of this equation is $n = 12$ or $n = -12$.
This is usually written as $n = \pm 12$. [you say 'n equals plus or minus twelve']

Now consider the equation $(x - 3)^2 = 16$.
Following the previous example, you can say that
$(x - 3) = 4$ or $(x - 3) = -4$.
So the solution of the equation is $x = 7$ or $x = -1$.

Finally, consider the equation $(y + 5)^2 = 33$.
As before, you take the square root of both sides of the equation:
$(y + 5) = 5.745$ or -5.745 (using a calculator)
   so $y = 0.745$ or $y = -10.745$

To solve quadratic equations by **completing the square** you have to know what number to add to $x^2 + kx$ to make it into a perfect square. You need it to be a perfect square so that you can write it as $(x + b)^2 = a$ and then you can solve it like the examples above.

The clue is in the result $x^2 + 2ax + a^2 = (x + a)^2$.

If $k = 2a$ then $a = \frac{k}{2}$ and the number to be added $= a^2$ which is $(\frac{k}{2})^2$.

This is easier than it sounds. Look at some examples.

Examples and solutions

1. To make $x^2 + 6x$ into a perfect square, add $(\frac{6}{2})^2 = 3^2 = 9$.

   Check: $x^2 + 6x + 9 = (x + 3)(x + 3) = (x + 3)^2$.

2. To make $x^2 - 20x$ into a perfect square, add
   $(\frac{-20}{2})^2 = (-10)^2 = 100$.

   Check: $x^2 - 20x + 100 = (x - 10)(x - 10) = (x - 10)^2$.

3. To make $x^2 + 7x$ into a perfect square, add $(\frac{7}{2})^2 = \frac{49}{4}$.

   Check: $x^2 + 7x + \frac{49}{4} = (x + \frac{7}{2})(x + \frac{7}{2}) = (x + \frac{7}{2})^2$.

4. To make $x^2 - \frac{1}{2}x$ into a perfect square, add $(\frac{-\frac{1}{2}}{2})^2 = \frac{1}{16}$.

   Check: $x^2 - \frac{1}{2}x + \frac{1}{16} = (x - \frac{1}{4})(x - \frac{1}{4}) = (x - \frac{1}{4})^2$.

> Dividing by 2 is the same as multiplying by its reciprocal, $\frac{1}{2}$.
> So $\frac{-\frac{1}{2}}{2} = -\frac{1}{2} \div 2 = -\frac{1}{2} \times \frac{1}{2} = -\frac{1}{4}$.

You are now in a position to solve quadratic equations by the method of completing the square. Watch carefully to see how it's done and then try the examples on your own to make sure you've really understood.

Example 1

Solve the quadratic equation $x^2 + 6x - 7 = 0$ by completing the square.

Solution

Rearrange the equation so that the terms containing x are alone on one side of the equation: $x^2 + 6x = 7$

> you can add *anything* to one side of an equation as long as you add the same thing to the other side

Complete the square by
adding $(\frac{6}{2})^2$ to each side: $x^2 + 6x + (\frac{6}{2})^2 = 7 + (\frac{6}{2})^2$

so $x^2 + 6x + 9 = 7 + 9$

that is $(x + 3)^2 = 16$

Take the square root of both sides: $(x + 3) = 4$ or -4

so $x = 1$ or $x = -7$

Example 2

Solve the quadratic equation $u^2 = 20u + 12$ by completing the square.

Solution

Rearrange the equation so that the terms containing u are alone on one side of the equation: $\qquad u^2 - 20u = 12$

Complete the square by adding
$(\frac{-20}{2})^2 = 100$ to each side: $\qquad u^2 - 20u + 100 = 12 + 100$
$$\text{that is } (u - 10)^2 = 112$$
Taking the square root of both sides: $(u - 10) = 10.583$ or -10.583
$$\text{so } u = 20.583 \text{ or}$$
$$u = -0.583$$

Example 3

Solve the quadratic equation $2x^2 - x = 5$ by completing the square.

Solution

Before completing the square, you must divide both sides of the equation by 2 so that there is a single x^2.

Divide both sides by 2: $\qquad x^2 - \frac{1}{2}x = \frac{5}{2}$

Complete the square by adding $(-\frac{1}{2} \times \frac{1}{2})^2 = \frac{1}{16}$ to each side:
$$x^2 - \frac{1}{2}x + \frac{1}{16} = \frac{5}{2} + \frac{1}{16}$$
$$\text{that is } (x - \frac{1}{4})^2 = \frac{41}{16}$$
Take the square root of both sides: $\qquad (x - \frac{1}{4}) = \frac{6.403}{4}$ or $\frac{-6.403}{4}$
$$\text{so } x = \frac{7.403}{4} \text{ or } \frac{-5.403}{4}$$
$$x = 1.851 \text{ or } -1.351 \text{ (correct to 3 decimal places)}$$

You should now answer a few questions on the method of completing the square. Remember the following things:

- divide throughout by the number in front of the squared term if it isn't 1
- the constant term must be on the R.H.S and the other terms on the L.H.S
- now complete the square.

EXERCISE 27

1. Find the number which has to be added to each of the following expressions to make it a perfect square. In each case, show that your answer is correct by factorising the resulting expression.
    a) $x^2 - 8x$ b) $y^2 + 10y$
    c) $t^2 + 3t$ d) $u^2 + \frac{2}{3}u$

2. Solve the quadratic equations by completing the square.
    a) $x^2 - 8x = 9$ b) $y^2 + 10y + 16 = 0$
    c) $t^2 + 3t = 1$ d) $3u^2 + 2u = 7$

Solving quadratic equations by formula

The method of completing the square can be used to obtain a formula for solving quadratic equations. Many learners prefer to use the formula rather than the original method of completing the square, but completing the square is used in other parts of mathematics, for example in calculus, and you should try to master it if you wish to study mathematics to a higher level.

Proof of the Formula It is NOT necessary for you to learn this proof. If you do not wish to see how the formula is obtained, proceed immediately to the examples of the use of the formula.

The general quadratic equation is: $\qquad ax^2 + bx + c = 0$

Subtract c from both sides: $\qquad\qquad\qquad ax^2 + bx = -c$

Divide both sides by a (so there is one x^2): $\quad x^2 + \dfrac{b}{a}\,x = \dfrac{-c}{a}$

Add $(\dfrac{b}{2a})^2$ to both sides (complete the square):

$$x^2 + \frac{b}{a}\,x + \left(\frac{b}{2a}\right)^2 \;=\; \frac{-c}{a} + \frac{b^2}{4a^2}$$

$$\text{That is } \left(x + \frac{b}{2a}\right)^2 = \frac{-4ac + b^2}{4a^2}$$

so, $(x + \dfrac{b}{2a}) = \dfrac{\sqrt{b^2 - 4ac}}{2a}$ or $\dfrac{-\sqrt{b^2 - 4ac}}{2a}$

The answers to the equation are $\quad x = \dfrac{-b + \sqrt{b^2 - 4ac}}{2a}$

$$\text{or } x = \frac{-b - \sqrt{b^2 - 4ac}}{2a}.$$

The quadratic equation formula is usually written as follows:

> If $ax^2 + bx + c = 0$, then $x = \dfrac{-b \pm \sqrt{b^2 - 4ac}}{2a}$.

Learn this formula very well. You will need to use it a lot.

Note that there are two answers to the equation. The symbol $\pm$ means 'plus or minus'. One answer is obtained by using the '+' sign and the other answer is obtained by using the '−' sign.

Example I

Solve the equation $2x^2 + 7x + 3 = 0$ by using the formula.

Solution

Comparing with $ax^2 + bx + c = 0$, we see that $a = 2$, $b = 7$, $c = 3$. It is useful to work out the value of ac here: $\quad ac = 2 \times 3 = 6$

Using the formula: $\quad x = \dfrac{-b \pm \sqrt{b^2 - 4ac}}{2a}$

$$x = \frac{-7 \pm \sqrt{49 - 4(6)}}{4} = \frac{-7 \pm \sqrt{49 - 24}}{4}$$

$$x = \frac{-7 \pm \sqrt{25}}{4}$$

$$x = \frac{-7 + 5}{4} \text{ or } \frac{-7 - 5}{4}$$

$$x = \frac{-2}{4} \quad \text{ or } \frac{-12}{4}$$

$$x = -\frac{1}{2} \quad \text{ or } -3$$

Example 2

Solve the equation $y^2 = 2y + 1$.

Solution

First rearrange the equation so that it is in the required form:

$$y^2 - 2y - 1 = 0$$

see that $\quad a = 1, b = -2, c = -1$

and $\quad ac = 1 \times (-1) = -1$

Using the formula: $y = \dfrac{-b \pm \sqrt{b^2 - 4ac}}{2a}$

$$= \dfrac{-(-2) \pm \sqrt{4 - 4(-1)}}{2}$$

$$= \dfrac{+2 \pm \sqrt{4 + 4}}{2}$$

$$= \dfrac{+2 \pm \sqrt{8}}{2}$$

using the calculator:

2 ⊞ 8 √ ⊟ ÷ 2 ⊟

or if you have a D.A.L. calculator:

2 ⊞ √ 8 ⊟ ÷ 2 ⊟

$$= \dfrac{+2 + 2.828}{2} \quad \text{or} \quad \dfrac{+2 - 2.828}{2}$$

$$= \dfrac{4.828}{2} \qquad \text{or} \qquad \dfrac{-0.828}{2}$$

$$= 2.41 \qquad\qquad \text{or} -0.41 \text{ (to 2 decimal places)}$$

Example 3

A ball is thrown vertically upwards. Its height above the ground, h metres, at time t seconds is given by $h = 24t - 5t^2$.

a) Calculate the height of the ball 3 seconds after being thrown.

b) At what time is the ball 20 m above the ground?

Solution

a) When $t = 3$, $h = 72 - 5(9) = 72 - 45 = 27$.
    After 3 seconds, the height of the ball is 27 m.

b) When $h = 20$, $\qquad\qquad 20 = 24t - 5t^2$
    Rearranging $\qquad 5t^2 - 24t + 20 = 0$
    Comparing with $\quad at^2 + bt + c = 0$,
    we see that $\quad a = 5, b = -24, c = -20$ and $ac = 100$.

Using the formula: $\quad t = \dfrac{-b \pm \sqrt{b^2 - 4ac}}{2a}$

$$= \dfrac{+24 \pm \sqrt{576 - 400}}{10}$$

$$= \dfrac{+24 \pm \sqrt{176}}{10}$$

$$t = \dfrac{+24 + 13.266}{10} \quad \text{or} \quad \dfrac{+24 - 13.266}{10}$$

$$= \dfrac{37.266}{10} \qquad \text{or} \qquad \dfrac{10.734}{10}$$

$$= 3.727 \qquad\qquad \text{or} \quad 1.073$$

The ball is at a height of 20 m on two occasions:
after 1.07 seconds and after 3.73 seconds.
(On the first occasion it is moving upwards. On the second occasion it is moving downwards.)

You must now practise using the quadratic equation formula by solving the following problems.

EXERCISE 28

1. Solve the quadratic equations using the formula.
    a) $5x^2 + 9x + 2 = 0$
    b) $y^2 = 4y + 1$
    c) $t^2 + t - 3 = 0$

2. Use the formula to solve the equations.
    a) $n^2 = 5n - 3$
    b) $x^2 - 6x - 21 = 0$
    c) $3m^2 + m - 1 = 0$

3. A picture has a length of L cm and a breadth of B cm.
    For the picture to be a pleasing shape, L and B should be related by $B(B + L) = L^2$.
    If the breadth of the picture is 30 cm, calculate the required length.

Check your answers at the end of this module.

Did you find that using the formula was easier than completing the square? It should be. But only if you remember the formula correctly. So make sure you have memorised it well before you continue with the last section of this unit.

C Solving simple linear inequalities

In this unit, and in Unit 1, we have considered the solution of equations. These are statements that two expressions are equal. In mathematics and in everyday life, we often meet statements about expressions that are *not* equal.

For example,   'Daniel is older than Zodwa'
                   'On this road, the speed of a car must not exceed 100 km/h'
                   'I want to buy at least 3 presents but the cost must not be more than R50'

When written in algebraic language, these statements contain one or more of the symbols $<$, $\leq$, $>$, $\geq$ and we call them **inequalities**.

Examples

1. 'Nobantu is under 21 years of age.'
    If we let Nobantu's age be x years, this statement would be written as $x < 21$.

2. 'On this road, the speed of a car must not exceed 100 km/h'.
    To put this statement into mathematical symbols, it is necessary to understand that 'the speed must not exceed 100 km/h' means that the speed must be 100 km/h or less.
    If we let the speed of the car be v km/h, the statement would be written as $v \leq 100$.

3. 'The bus service will operate if the number of passengers is more than 30.' If we let the number of passengers be n, this statement would be written $n > 30$.

4. 'To go to the party, children must be between 5 and 10 years of age.' This is really two statements in one:
    'children must be more than 5 years old'
    and 'children must be less than 10 years old'.
    If we let a child's age be y years, these would be written $y > 5$ and $y < 10$. Such statements are often written in the form $5 < y < 10$.
    It is essential that you remember that here there are two inequalities to be satisfied simultaneously. The inequality signs *must* be the same way round: you must *never* write algebraic statements such as $5 > y < 10$ or $5 < y > 10$.

Representing inequalities on a number line

Inequalities can be illustrated by drawing a line above or below a number line. The line extends over all the numbers which satisfy the inequality.

If the inequality involves $<$ or $>$, the end point of the line is not part of the solution and this is indicated by drawing a hollow circle at the end of the line.

If the inequality involves $\leq$ or $\geq$, the end point of the line is part of the solution and this is indicated by drawing a filled-in circle at the end of the line.

Example 1

Represent the inequality $x < 3$ on a number line.

Solution

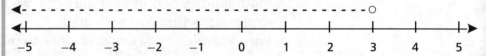

Note that $x = 3$ does not satisfy the inequality so a hollow circle is drawn above $x = 3$. The arrow head indicates that the line extends indefinitely to the left.

Example 2

Represent the inequality $x \geq -2$ on a number line.

Solution

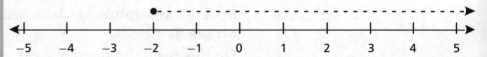

Note that $x = -2$ does satisfy the inequality so a filled-in circle is drawn above $x = -2$. The arrow head indicates that the line extends indefinitely to the right.

Example 3

Represent the inequality $-2 \leq x < 3$ on a number line.

Solution

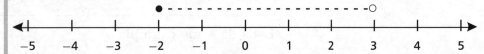

This is a combination of Examples 1 and 2. All numbers between -2 and 3 satisfy the inequality and so does $x = -2$. However, $x = 3$ does not satisfy the inequality.

Example 4

Write down the inequality represented by the number line below.

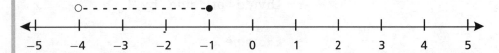

Solution

All numbers between -4 and -1 satisfy the inequality and, taking into account the filled-in circle, so does $x = -1$. The hollow circle at $x = -4$ indicates that $x = -4$ does not satisfy the inequality. The number line therefore represents the inequality $-4 < x \leq -1$.

> you say 'x is greater than -4 *and* x is less than or equal to -1'

Solving linear inequalities

The rules for solving inequalities such as $2x + 1 > 15$, $3(y - 2) < 21$ and $4t - 3 \geq 6t + 1$ are very similar to those we used for solving equations such as $2x + 1 = 15$, $3(y - 2) = 21$ and $4t - 3 = 6t + 1$. There are, however, some important exceptions concerning multiplication and division.

You can do any of the following to an inequality:

- add the same number or expression to both sides
- subtract the same number or expression from both sides
- multiply both sides by the same POSITIVE number or expression
- divide both sides by the same POSITIVE number or expression.

But look at what happens when you multiply both sides of an inequality by a negative number.

Do you agree that $10 > 5$?

Now multiply both sides by a negative number. Any negative number.

I'll multiply by -2: $-20 > -10$. Is this still true?

Think of the number line. No! $-20 < -10$. That's why we have a rule:

> If you multiply both sides of an inequality by a negative number the inequality sign *changes direction*.

What about if you divide both sides by a negative number? Try it yourself. I hope you agree that the same rule would apply:

> If you divide both sides of an inequality by a negative number the inequality sign *changes direction*.

Let's do some examples.

Example 1

Solve the inequality $2x + 1 > 15$

Solution

$$2x + 1 > 15$$

Subtract 1 from both sides: $\quad 2x > 14$
Divide both sides by 2: $\quad x > 7$

Example 2

Solve the inequality $\frac{2y - 1}{3} \le 4$.

Solution

$$\frac{2y - 1}{3} \le 4$$

Multiply both sides by 3: $\quad 2y - 1 \le 12$
Add 1 to both sides: $\quad 2y \le 13$
Divide both sides by 2: $\quad y \le 6.5$

Example 3

Solve the inequality $2t + 3 > 7t + 11$.

Solution

$$2t + 3 > 7t + 11$$

Subtract $7t$ from both sides: $-5t + 3 > 11$
Subtract 3 from both sides: $\quad -5t > 8$
Divide both sides by -5: $\quad t < -\frac{8}{5}$

> if you divide by a negative number the sign changes direction

The solution of the inequality is $t < -1.6$.

Example 4

Solve the inequality $-5 \le 2x + 1 < 5$.

Solution

(There are two inequalities here. Deal with them separately.)
For the inequality: $\quad -5 \le 2x + 1 \quad$ ①
$$-6 \le 2x$$
$$-3 \le x$$
For the inequality: $\quad 2x + 1 < 5 \quad$ ②
$$2x < 4$$
$$x < 2$$

Both inequalities ① and ② must be satisfied, so the solution required is $-3 \le x < 2$.

Example 5

Find the two integer values of t which satisfy all these conditions:
$2t + 6 \geq 0$, $t \neq -2$, $t < 0$.

Solution

The inequality $2t + 6 \geq 0$ gives $2t \geq -6$ and so $t \geq -3$.
Using the inequality $t < 0$, we deduce that $-3 \leq t < 0$.
However, we are told that t is an integer and that it is
not equal to -2.
The two required values of t are, therefore, -3 and -1.

EXERCISE 29

1. Solve the inequalities:
   a) $3x + 7 > 1$
   b) $\dfrac{5y - 3}{4} < 8$
   c) $3 - 5t \geq 18$

2. Solve the inequality $-3 \leq 2x + 3 < 3$ and illustrate
   your solution on a number line.

3. Given that n is a positive integer, list the values of n for which
   $-8 \leq 4n < 10$.

4. Given that x is a positive integer, $x \leq 5$ and $x \neq 3$, list the
   possible values of x.

Check your answers at the end of this module.

Summary

In this unit you learnt two different methods for solving
simultaneous equations:

- the substitution method
- the method of equal coefficients.

To solve quadratic equations you made use of the important fact
that:

- if two numbers multiplied together give 0, then one of the
  numbers *must* be 0.

You also learnt two other methods for solving quadratic equations
besides factorising:

- completing the square
- using the formula $x = \dfrac{-b \pm \sqrt{b^2 - 4ac}}{2a}$.

You saw that the rules for solving inequalities are the same as for solving equations, except for one important difference:

- if you multiply or divide both sides of an inequality by a negative (−) number the inequality sign *changes direction*.

That's it for Module 2. With the basic skills of algebra you've mastered in this module you'll be able to draw the graphs in Module 3. Remember that the more practice you get the easier it becomes. So don't be shy to go over the examples and exercises in this module again – remember, don't just read, work with a pencil and paper.

Check your progress

1. Solve the simultaneous equations: $3x - y = 11$
$$4x + y = 10.$$

2. The pressure P at a depth x metres below the surface of the ocean is given by the formula $P = ax + b$, where a and b are constants.
   When $x = 0$, $P = 15$.
   When $x = 60$, $P = 45$.

   a)   Find the values of a and b.
   b)   Hence, or otherwise, calculate the pressure at a depth of 100 m.

3. Consider these statements about two digit numbers:

   $$\boxed{3 \mid 7} = 10 \times 3 + 7$$
   $$\boxed{5 \mid 3} = 10 \times 5 + 3$$

   a)   Fill in the blanks in this statement:

   $$\boxed{2 \mid 9} = \ldots\ldots + \ldots\ldots$$

   b)   If $\boxed{p \mid q}$ represents a two digit number (like 37) then
   $\boxed{p \mid q} = 10p + q$.

   (i)   Complete the statement $\boxed{q \mid p} = \ldots\ldots + \ldots\ldots$

   (ii)   Show that $\boxed{p \mid q} - \boxed{q \mid p} = 9p - 9q$.

   c)   A two digit number $\boxed{p \mid q}$ is such that
   $$\boxed{p \mid q} - \boxed{q \mid p} = 18.$$

   (i)   Use the result in part b) (ii) to write down an equation in p and q.
   (ii)   It is also given that $p + q = 14$.
   Solve these simultaneous equations to find p and q.
   (iii)   Write down the two digit number.

4. Solve the quadratic equation $(2y + 5)^2 = 49$.

5. The formula connecting the variables x and y is $y = \frac{a}{x} + bx$.
   It is known that $y = 2$ when $x = 1$ and that $y = -5$ when $x = 2$.
   a) Find the value of a and the value of b.
   b) Show that when $y = 16$, the formula $y = \frac{a}{x} + bx$ becomes
      $2x^2 + 8x - 3 = 0$.
   c) Solve the equation $2x^2 + 8x - 3 = 0$, giving your answers
      correct to 2 decimal places.

6. Solve the inequality $7 < 3 - 2x \leq 13$ and represent your answer
   on a number line.

7. It is given that $-5 \leq x \leq -3$ and $-1 \leq y \leq 2$.
   Find the largest possible value of:
   a) $x + y$
   b) xy
   c) x^2y

Check your answers at the end of this module.

Solutions

EXERCISE 1

1. $P = L \times 2 + B \times 2$. This is usually written
   as $P = 2L + 2B$.
   L units is the length of the rectangle.
   B units is the breadth and
   P units is the perimeter.

2. $a + b = b + a$

3. Multiplying n by 5 and taking away 8 gives the same
   answer as adding 20 to n.

4. a) $n \times 3 - 7 = n + 5$. This is usually written
      as $3n - 7 = n + 5$.
   b) The only value of n for which this is true is 6.
      (If you could not see that n has to be 6, don't
      worry – I'll show you how to solve equations
      in Section B.)

5. $k \times k - 3 = 2k$
   This is usually written as $k^2 - 3 = 2k$.

EXERCISE 2

1. a) $p^2 - q^2 = 6^2 - 2^2 = 36 - 4 = 32$
   b) $(p - q)^2 = (6 - 2)^2 = 4^2 = 16$

2. a) $x - (y + z) = 5 - (2 + 3) = 5 - 5 = 0$
   b) $x - y + z = 5 - 2 + 3 = 3 + 3 = 6$

3. a) $b > y$
   b) $b = 2y$

4. $n^2 \times 2 - 15 = 377$ or $2n^2 - 15 = 377$

5. $A = \frac{D \times d \times \pi}{4}$ or $A = \frac{\pi D d}{4}$

   where A = area of the ellipse
   D = length of the major diameter
   d = length of the minor diameter

   > You may have used different letters. It is important
   > that you state what your letters represent.

EXERCISE 3

1. a) $P = 2 \times 12 + 2 \times 7$
      $= 24 + 14$
      $= 38$
   b) $P = 2(4.6) + 2(3.5)$
      $= 9.2 + 7.0$
      $= 16.2$

2. $d = \frac{100(100 + 32)}{150} = \frac{100 \times 132}{150}$

   $= \frac{2 \times 132}{3}$

   $= \frac{2 \times 44}{1}$

   $= 88$

3. a) $C = 12 \times 5 + 750$
      $= 60 + 750$
      $= 810$
   b) $C = 12 \times 500 + 750$
      $= 6000 + 750$
      $= 6750$

4. $d = 3.55 \times \sqrt{32}$
   $= 3.55 \times 5.65685$
   $= 20.08183 \ldots$

   > use your calculator to find
   > the square root of 32

   The distance to the horizon is
   20.1 km (to 3 significant figures).

5. Area of the base = 5×5 cm^2 + 25 cm^2.

   Volume of pyramid = $25 \times 6 \div 3$
   $= 150 \div 3$
   $= 50$ cm^3.

EXERCISE 4

1. $2n + 7n - 3n = 6n$
    a) $6(8) = 48$
    b) $6(72) = 432$

2. a) $p + 2q$
    b) $7n - 3$
    c) $2x^3 + 2x^2 + 5x$
    d) No like terms so the expression
        stays $3xy - 3 + y$.
    e) $-c - 4d$
    f) $x^2 - 3x + 6$

3. a) $16x - 12$
    b) $14n + 35$
    c) $48 - 16y$
    d) $6x^2 + 9x - 15$
    e) $30pq - 6p - 12q$

4. a) $3n + 15 + 8n - 12 = 11n + 3$
    b) $14x - 7 + 6 - 2x = 12x - 1$
    c) $5y - 3 + 12y - 6 = 17y - 9$
    d) $12c + 10d + 6d - 12c = 16d$
    e) $8x^2 + 8x - 24 + 10 - 5x = 8x^2 + 3x - 14$

EXERCISE 5

1. $5x + 3 = 38$
    $5x = 38 - 3$
    $5x = 35$
    so $x = 7$

2. $4n - 1 = n + 8$
    $4n - n = 8 + 1$
    $3n = 9$
    so $n = 3$

3. $6(x + 2) = 42$
    Method A: $x + 2 = 7$ [divide both sides by 6]
         so $x = 7 - 2 = 5$
    Method B: $6(x + 2) = 42$ [remove brackets]
         $6x + 12 = 42$
         so $6x = 42 - 12$
         $6x = 30$
         so $x = 5$

4. $7(y - 3) + 5 = 4(2 - y) + 3y$
    $7y - 21 + 5 = 8 - 4y + 3y$
    $7y - 16 = 8 - y$
    $8y - 16 = 8$
    $8y = 24$
    so $y = 3$

5. The equation is $3n + 2 = 50 - n$.

    Now solve it: $4n + 2 = 50$
           $4n = 48$
         so $n = 12$

6. a) $C = \frac{1}{2}(70) - 15 = 35 - 15 = 20$
    b) $30 = \frac{1}{2}F - 15$
        so $45 = \frac{1}{2}F$
        and so $90 = F$
        that is $F = 90$

        [it's always best to get rid of fractions in equations by *multiplying* **both** sides by the LCM of the denominators]

EXERCISE 6

1. a) $47 = 3x + 8$
        $47 - 8 = 3x$
        $39 = 3x$
        The required answer is $x = 13$.

    b) $y = 3x + 8$
        $y - 8 = 3x$
        $\frac{y - 8}{3} = x$
        The required answer is $x = \frac{y - 8}{3}$.

2. a) $4x + 5 = 17$
        $4x = 12$
        so $x = 3$

    b) $ax + b = c$
        $ax = c - b$
        $x = \frac{c - b}{a}$

3. $v = u + at$
    $v - at = u$
    so $u = v - at$

4. $P = \frac{1}{2}W + 6$
    $P - 6 = \frac{1}{2}W$ [remember to multiply the *whole* side by 2]
    $2(P - 6) = W$

    The required formula is $W = 2(P - 6)$.
    This could be written as $W = 2P - 12$.

5. $2x + 3y = 12$
    $3y = 12 - 2x$
    $y = \frac{12 - 2x}{3}$ is the required formula.

6. $C = 2\pi r$
    $\frac{C}{2\pi} = r$
    The formula required is $r = \frac{C}{2\pi}$.

EXERCISE 6 (cont.)

7.　$S = \sqrt{1.5H}$　　square both sides
$S^2 = 1.5H$

$\dfrac{S^2}{1.5} = H$

The formula
required is $H = \dfrac{S^2}{1.5}$　$\boxed{1.5 = \frac{3}{2} \text{ so } \frac{1}{1.5} = \frac{2}{3}}$

which is $H = \dfrac{2S^2}{3}$

8.　　$E = \dfrac{Wv^2}{2g}$

$2gE = Wv^2$

$\dfrac{2gE}{W} = v^2$

$\pm\sqrt{\dfrac{2gE}{W}} = v$

The required formula is $v = \pm\sqrt{\dfrac{2gE}{W}}$.

EXERCISE 7

1.　Let Jan's present age be n years.
In 7 years' time he will be $(n + 7)$ years old.
8 years ago he was $(n - 8)$ years old.
In 7 years' time Jan will be twice as old as he
was 8 years ago.
We can therefore write the equation:
$$(n + 7) = 2(n - 8)$$
$$\text{so } n + 7 = 2n - 16$$
$$n + 23 = 2n$$
$$23 = n$$
Jan's present age is 23 years.

(Check: In 7 years' time he will be 30 years old and
8 years ago he was 15 years old.
This fits the facts because $30 = 2 \times 15$.)

2.　Let Sipho's age be n years.
Then Temba's age is $2n$ years and Silo's age
is $(n - 5)$ years.
The total of their ages is 31 years.
We can therefore write the equation:
$$n + 2n + (n - 5) = 31$$
$$4n - 5 = 31$$
$$4n = 36$$
$$n = 9$$
Sipho is 9 years old.

(Check: Temba is 18 years old and Silo is 4 years old.
This fits the facts because $9 + 18 + 4 = 31$.)

3.　Let the weight of the middle piece be x grams.
Then the weight of the largest piece is $(x + 7)$ grams
and the weight of the smallest piece is $(x - 4)$ grams.
The whole pizza weighed 300 g.
We can therefore write the equation:
$$x + (x + 7) + (x - 4) = 300$$
$$3x + 3 = 300$$
$$3x = 297$$
$$x = 99$$
The middle piece weighs 99 g the largest piece weighs
106 g and the smallest piece weighs 95 g.

(Check: This fits the facts because
$99 + 106 + 95 = 300$.)

4.　Let the distance Herman rowed upstream be
d kilometres.
Upstream Herman travels at $(8 - 2)$ km/h = 6 km/h
so time taken = $\dfrac{d}{6}$ hours.　$\boxed{\text{time} = \dfrac{\text{distance}}{\text{speed}}}$

Downstream Herman travels
at $(8 + 2)$ km/h = 10 km/h so time taken = $\dfrac{d}{10}$ hours.

Altogether the journey took 2 hours.

We can therefore write the equation:
$$\dfrac{d}{6} + \dfrac{d}{10} = 2$$
$$5d + 3d = 60 \quad \boxed{\begin{array}{l}\text{LCM of denominators} = 30 \\ \text{multiply both sides by } 30\end{array}}$$
$$8d = 60$$
$$d = 7.5$$
Herman rowed 7.5 km upstream.

(Check: 7.5 km at 6 km/h takes 1.25 hours and
7.5 km at 10 km/h takes 0.75 hours.
This fits the facts because
1.25 hours + 0.75 hours = 2 hours.)

5.　Let the number of times Dickson bought a ticket for a
seat be n.
Then the number of times he bought a ticket to stand
is $(21 - n)$.
The n tickets for a seat cost $45n$ Rand.
The $(21 - n)$ tickets to stand cost $25(21 - n)$ Rand.
The total cost was R765 so we can write:
$$45n + 25(21 - n) = 765$$
$$\text{so } 45n + 525 - 25n = 765$$
$$20n + 525 = 765$$
$$20n = 240$$
$$n = 12$$
Dickson bought a ticket for a seat 12 times.

(Check: 12 tickets at R45 each cost R540 and 9 tickets
at R25 each cost R225.
This fits the facts because
R540 + R225 = R765.)

EXERCISE 8

1. The numbers increase by 2 so there will be $2n$ in the sequence. Using $2n$ the sequence is 2, 4, 6, 8, 10, . . . Add 3 to each term to get the required sequence. So the formula for the nth term is $2n + 3$.

2. The numbers increase by 3 so there will be $3n$ in the sequence. Using $3n$ the sequence is 3, 6, 9, 12, 15, . . . Subtract 1 from each term to get the required sequence. So the formula for the nth term is $3n - 1$.

3. The numbers decrease by 2 so there will be $-2n$ in the sequence. Using $-2n$ the sequence is -2, -4, -6, -8, -10, . . . Add 14 to each term to get the required sequence. So the formula for the nth term is $-2n + 14$ which can be written as $14 - 2n$.

4. The numbers increase by $\frac{1}{2}$ so there will be $\frac{1}{2}n$ in the sequence. Using $\frac{1}{2}n$ the sequence is $\frac{1}{2}$, 1, $1\frac{1}{2}$, 2, $2\frac{1}{2}$, . . . Add 1 to each term to get the required sequence. So the formula for the nth term is $\frac{1}{2}n + 1$.

5. The numbers do not increase or decrease by the same amount each time so the answer must be obtained 'by inspection'. The numbers in the sequence are the cube numbers so the formula for the nth term is n^3.

EXERCISE 9

1. $A = kr^2$ and $r = 3$ when $A = 36$ means that $36 = k(3^2)$. So $k = 4$. From $A = 4r^2$ it follows that, when $r = 10$, $A = 400$.

2. $I = \frac{k}{d^3}$ and $I = 100$ when $d = 2$.
so $100 = \frac{k}{2^3}$
$k = 800$
From $I = \frac{800}{d^3}$ it follows that, when $d = 5$,
$I = \frac{800}{125} = 6.4$

3. $2 \times 75 = 150$, $5 \times 30 = 150$, $8 \times 20 = 160$, $12 \times 15 = 180$. These products of corresponding values of p and q are not all equal so p and q are *not* inversely proportional.

4. $I = \frac{k}{R}$ and $I = 5$ when $R = 3$.
so $3 \times 5 = k$
$k = 15$
From $I = \frac{15}{R}$ it follows that, when $R = 0.25$,
$I = \frac{15}{0.25} = 60$.

5. The values fit $t \propto s^3$.
From the table

s^3	8	216	1000
t	0.4	10.8	50

we can deduce $t = \frac{s^3}{20}$ and k in this case is $\frac{1}{20}$.

Check your progress 1

1. a) $c + w + m = 14$
   b) $c > 3$
   c) $m \neq c$
   d) $w = m + 2$

2. $\sqrt{\frac{(5.3)^2 + (4.8)^2}{6}} = \sqrt{\frac{51.13}{6}} = 2.919189385$
   $= 2.92$ to 3 significant figures.

3. a) $S = 13 + 14 = 27$
   b) $48 = 13 + 5R$
   $35 = 5R$
   so $R = 7$
   c) $S = 13 + 5R$
   $S - 13 = 5R$
   so $R = \frac{S - 13}{5}$

4. a) $4x = 34$
   $x = \frac{34}{4} = 8.5$
   b) $y = \frac{15}{4} = 3.75$
   c) $5z + 10 = 3z - 3 + 23$
   $5z + 10 = 3z + 20$
   $2z + 10 = 20$
   $2z = 10$
   $z = 5$

Check your progress 1 (cont.)

5. a)

number of squares in line	1	2	3	4	5	6	7	8
number of match-sticks needed	4	7	10	13	16	19	22	25

b) 19

c) Each term in the sequence increases by 3. So there will be $3n$ in the formula. Using $3n$ the sequence is $3, 6, 9, 12, \ldots$ Add 1 to get the correct sequence. So the formula is $3n + 1$.

6. a) $3x + 2y = 20$

b) Driver must make a whole number of journeys with each truck.

c) $x = 2$ and $y = 7$ $x = 4$ and $y = 4$
$x = 6$ and $y = 1$

7. $y = \frac{k}{x^2}$ and $y = 1.5$ when $x = 12$

Hence, $1.5 = \frac{k}{144}$ and $k = 1.5 \times 144 = 216$

$y = \frac{216}{x^2}$ so, when $x = 3$, $y = \frac{216}{9} = 24$

EXERCISE 10

1. a) $2^3 \times 5^3 = (2 \times 2 \times 2) \times (5 \times 5 \times 5) = 8 \times 125 \times 1000$ (or $2^3 \times 5^3 = 10^3 = 1000$)

b) $2^8 \div 8^2 = (2 \times 2 \times 2 \times 2 \times 2 \times 2 \times 2 \times 2) \div (8 \times 8) = 256 \div 64 = 4$

c) $(\frac{3}{5})^4 = \frac{3}{5} \times \frac{3}{5} \times \frac{3}{5} \times \frac{3}{5} = \frac{81}{625}$

d) $1^8 = 1 \times 1 \times 1 \times 1 \times 1 \times 1 \times 1 \times 1 = 1$

2. a) $4^2 \times 4^3 = (4 \times 4) \times (4 \times 4 \times 4) = 16 \times 64 = 1024$

b) $4^5 = 4 \times 4 \times 4 \times 4 \times 4 = 1024$

c) $6^3 \times 6 = (6 \times 6 \times 6) \times 6 = 216 \times 6 = 1296$

d) $6^4 = 6 \times 6 \times 6 \times 6 = 1296$

3. a) $3^5 \div 3^3 = (3 \times 3 \times 3 \times 3 \times 3) \div (3 \times 3 \times 3) = 243 \div 27 = 9$

b) $3^2 = 9$

c) $10^6 \div 10^4 = 1\,000\,000 \div 10\,000 = 100$

d) $10^2 = 100$

4. a) $(1.1)^4 = (1.1) \times (1.1) \times (1.1) \times (1.1) = 1.4641$

b) $(3^2)^3 = (3^2) \times (3^2) \times (3^2) = 9 \times 9 \times 9 = 729$

c) $(3^3)^2 = (3^3) \times (3^3) = 27 \times 27 = 729$

d) $(10^2)^4 = (10^2) \times (10^2) \times (10^2) \times (10^2) = 100 \times 100 \times 100 \times 100 = 100\,000\,000$

EXERCISE 11

1. a) $8^3 \times 8^2 = 8^{3 + 2} = 8^5$

b) $4^4 \times 4^4 = 4^{4 + 4} = 4^8$

c) $6^3 \times 6^2 \times 6^7 = 6^{3 + 2 + 7} = 6^{12}$

d) $5^3 \times 5^8 \times 5 = 5^3 \times 5^8 \times 5^1 = 5^{3 + 8 + 1} = 5^{12}$

2. a) $3^8 \div 3^2 = 3^{8 - 2} = 3^6$

b) $2^{20} \div 2^5 = 2^{20 - 5} = 2^{15}$

c) $4^6 \div 4^5 = 4^{6 - 5} = 4^1 = 4$

d) $7^7 \div 7 = 7^7 \div 7^1 = 7^{7 - 1} = 7^6$

3. a) $(5^2)^4 = 5^{2 \times 4} = 5^8$

b) $(5^4)^2 = 5^{4 \times 2} = 5^8$

c) $(9^8)^3 = 9^{8 \times 3} = 9^{24}$

d) $[(4^2)^3]^5 = [4^{2 \times 3}]^5 = [4^6]^5 = 4^{6 \times 5} = 4^{30}$

4. a) $2^6 \times 2^3 \div 2^4 = 2^{6 + 3} \div 2^4 = 2^9 \div 2^4 = 2^{9 - 4} = 2^5$

b) $6^3 \times 6^5 \div 6^7 = 6^{3 + 5} \div 6^7 = 6^8 \div 6^7 = 6^{8 - 7} = 6^1 = 6$

c) $(3^5 \div 3^3)^4 = (3^{5 - 3})^4 = (3^2)^4 = 3^{2 \times 4} = 3^8$

d) $(8^3)^3 \div 8^4 = 8^{3 \times 3} \div 8^4 = 8^9 \div 8^4 = 8^{9 - 4} = 8^5$

EXERCISE 12

1. a) $5g^4 = 5 \times g \times g \times g \times g = 5 \times 3 \times 3 \times 3 \times 3 = 405$

b) $g^2 h^3 = g \times g \times h \times h \times h = 3 \times 3 \times 4 \times 4 \times 4 = 576$

c) $2g^3 + h^3 = (2 \times g \times g \times g) + (h \times h \times h)$
$= (2 \times 3 \times 3 \times 3) + (4 \times 4 \times 4) = 54 + 64 = 118$

d) $3h^2 + 2h - 5 = (3 \times h \times h) + (2 \times h) - 5$
$= (3 \times 4 \times 4) + (2 \times 4) - 5 = 48 + 8 - 5 = 51$

EXERCISE 12 (cont.)

2. a) $4f^3 \times 3f^4 = (4 \times 3) \times (f^3 \times f^4) = 12 \times f^{3+4} = 12f^7$
    b) $5y^2 \times y^6 = 5 \times (y^2 \times y^6) = 5 \times y^{2+6} = 5y^8$
    c) $3e \times 2e^4 = (3 \times 2) \times (e^1 \times e^4) = 6 \times e^{1+4} = 6e^5$
    d) $7pq^2 \times 6p^2q = (7 \times 6) \times (p^1 \times p^2) \times (q^2 \times q^1)$
        $= 42 \times p^{1+2} \times q^{2+1}$
        $= 42p^3q^3$

3. a) $8p^8 \div 4p^4 = (8 \div 4) \times (p^8 \div p^4) = 2 \times p^{8-4} = 2p^4$
    b) $7q^5 \div q^4 = 7 \times (q^5 \div q^4) = 7 \times q^{5-4} = 7q^1 = 7q$
    c) $9y^3 \div 3y = (9 \div 3) \times (y^3 \div y^1) = 3 \times y^{3-1} = 3y^2$
    d) $8p^3q^2 \div 4pq = (8 \div 4) \times (p^3 \div p^1) \times (q^2 \div q^1)$
        $= 2 \times p^{3-1} \times q^{2-1}$
        $= 2p^2q^1$
        $= 2p^2q$

4. a) $(4k^2)^3 = (4k^2) \times (4k^2) \times (4k^2) = (4 \times 4 \times 4) \times (k^2 \times k^2 \times k^2) = 64k^{2+2+2} = 64k^6$
    b) $(3p^4)^2 = (3p^4) \times (3p^4) = (3 \times 3) \times (p^4 \times p^4) = 9 \times p^{4+4} = 9p^8$
    c) $q(3q^2 - 5q - 1) = 3q^1q^2 - 5qq - q = 3q^{1+2} - 5q^2 - q = 3q^3 - 5q^2 - q$
    d) $5y^4(y^2 + 2y - 7) = 5y^4y^2 + 10y^4y^1 - 35y^4 = 5y^6 + 10y^5 - 35y^4$

EXERCISE 13

1. a) $5^{-2} = \frac{1}{5^2} = \frac{1}{25}$

    b) $(0.0006)^0 = 1$

    c) $(\frac{2}{5})^{-3} = (\frac{5}{2})^3 = \frac{125}{8}$

    d) $4^{-1} \times 4^0 \times 4^3 = 4^{-1+0+3} = 4^2 = 16$

2. a) $y^6 \times y^{-2} = y^{6+(-2)} = y^4$
    b) $k^5 \times k \times k^{-6} = k^5 \times k^1 \times k^{-6} = k^0 = 1$
    c) $p^3 \div p^6 = p^{3-6} = p^{-3}$
    d) $q^4 \div q^{-2} = q^{4-(-2)} = q^{4+2} = q^6$

3. a) $e^6 \div e^2 = e^{6-2} = e^4$
    b) $e^6 \div e^{-2} = e^{6-(-2)} = e^{6+2} = e^8$

    c) $(2^{-1})^{-1} = (\frac{1}{2})^{-1} = 2$

    d) $k \div k^{-3} = k^1 \div k^{-3} = k^{1-(-3)} = k^{1+3} = k^4$

EXERCISE 14

1. a) 7.89×10^4
    b) 3.479×10^2
    c) 5.8×10^{-5}
    d) 1.234×10^{-1}

2. a) 120
    b) 0.0314
    c) 0.0007605
    d) 2 800 000 000

3. a) 4.8×10^{10}
    b) 1.44×10^4
    c) 1.6×10^4
    d) 5×10^{10}
    e) 7.28×10^5
    f) 9.83×10^{-1}
    g) 2.27×10^4
    h) 8.43×10^{-2}

EXERCISE 15

1. Time taken $= (1.496 \times 10^8) \div (2.998 \times 10^5)$ seconds
    $= 0.499 \times 10^3$ seconds
    $= 499$ seconds (to the nearest second)

2. Total area $= (9.191 \times 10^4) + (4.9259 \times 10^5)$ km^2
    $= (91\ 910) + (492\ 590)$
    $= 584\ 500$
    5.845×10^5 km^2

3. Difference between diameter
    $= (1.243 \times 10^{-3}) - (7.14 \times 10^{-4})$ cm
    $= (0.001243) - (0.000714)$ cm
    $= 0.000529$ cm
    $= 5.29 \times 10^{-4}$ cm

4. Population $= (1.2247 \times 10^5) \times 33.67$
    $= 4.1235649 \times 10^7$
    $= 4.12 \times 10^7$ to 3 significant figures.

EXERCISE 16

1. a) $16^{\frac{1}{2}} = \sqrt{16} = 4$
   b) $27^{\frac{2}{3}} = (\sqrt[3]{27})^2 = 3^2 = 9$
   c) $25^{\frac{3}{2}} = (\sqrt{25})^3 = 5^3 = 125$
   d) $10\,000^{0.75} = 10\,000^{\frac{3}{4}} = (\sqrt[4]{10\,000})^3$
      $= (10)^3 = 1000$

2. a) $(\frac{25}{4})^{\frac{3}{2}} = (\sqrt{\frac{25}{4}})^3 = (\frac{5}{2})^3 = \frac{125}{8}$
   b) $8^{\frac{1}{4}} \times 8^{\frac{1}{12}} = 8^{(\frac{1}{4} + \frac{1}{12})} = 8^{\frac{1}{3}} = \sqrt[3]{8} = 2$
   c) $9^{\frac{3}{4}} \div 9^{\frac{1}{4}} = 9^{(\frac{3}{4}) - (\frac{1}{4})} = 9^{\frac{1}{2}} = \sqrt{9} = 3$
   d) $32^{0.6} = 32^{\frac{3}{5}} = (\sqrt[5]{32})^3 = 2^3 = 8$

3. a) $27^{-\frac{2}{3}} = (\frac{1}{27})^{\frac{2}{3}} = (\sqrt[3]{\frac{1}{27}})^2 = (\frac{1}{3})^2 = \frac{1}{9}$
   b) $(\frac{9}{25})^{-\frac{3}{2}} = (\frac{25}{9})^{\frac{3}{2}} = \sqrt{\frac{25}{9}}^3 = (\frac{5}{3})^3 = \frac{125}{27}$
   c) $e^{-\frac{1}{2}} \div e^{-\frac{3}{2}} = e^{(-\frac{1}{2}) - (-\frac{3}{2})} = e^1 = e$
   d) $(f^{\frac{1}{2}})^6 = f^{(\frac{1}{2}) \times 6} = f^3$

Check your progress 2

1. a) $64 \times 25 = 1600$
   b) $64 + 8 + 1 = 73$
   c) $\frac{1}{5} + \frac{1}{25} = \frac{6}{25}$
   d) 300

2. a) $33.8 \times 10^4 < 2.7 \times 10^6$
   b) 2.7×10^6 is in standard form
   c) $33.8 \times 10^4 = (3.38 \times 10^1) \times 10^4$
      $= 3.38 \times 10^5$

3. a) $33p^2 \div 11p^{-4} = (33 \div 11) \times (p^{2 - (-4)}) = 3p^6$
   b) $(5q^{12})^2 = 5^2 q^{24} = 25q^{24}$
   c) $2y^2 \times 3y^{-5} = (2 \times 3) \times y^{2 - 5} = 6y^{-3}$

4. 1 day $= 60 \times 60 \times 24$ seconds
   1 year $= 60 \times 60 \times 24 \times 365.25$ seconds
      $= 31\,557\,600$ seconds
   Number of heartbeats
   in 70 years $= 31\,557\,600 \times 70$
      $= 2\,209\,032\,000$
      $= 2.21 \times 10^9$ (correct to 3 significant
      figures).

5. Area of film
   $= (4 \times 10^{10}) \div (1.5 \times 10^8)$ cm^2
   $= 2.66666 \times 10^2$ cm^2
   $= 266.666$ cm^2
   $= 267$ cm^2 (correct to 3 significant figures).

6. a) (i) $\qquad (16e^{10})^{-\frac{1}{2}}$
   $$= \frac{1}{(16e^{10})^{\frac{1}{2}}}$$
   $$= \frac{1}{\sqrt{16e^{10}}}$$
   $$= \frac{1}{4e^5}$$
   (ii) $\qquad 2p^{\frac{1}{2}} \times 3p^{-\frac{5}{2}}$
   $$= 6p^{\frac{1}{2} - \frac{5}{2}}$$
   $$= 6p^{-\frac{4}{2}}$$
   $$= 6p^{-2}$$
   $$= \frac{6}{p^2}$$
   b) (i) $3^x = 81$
      $x = 4$ because $3^4 = 81$
   (ii) $3^x = \frac{1}{9}$
      $3^x = \frac{1}{3^2}$
      $3^x = 3^{-2}$
      so $x = -2$
   (iii) $3^x = 1$
      $x = 0$ because $3^0 = 1$

EXERCISE 17

1. a) $(+9)$ b) (-1) c) $(+2)$
   d) (-7) c) (-6)

2. a) $(+7)$ b) $(+10)$ c) (-3)
   d) (-5) e) $(+9)$

3. a) You should do the calculation from left to right:
   $(+2) + (+3) + (+4) = (+5) + (+4) = (+9)$
   b) You should first change any subtractions into additions:
   $(-6) + (+5) - (-7) = (-6) + (+5) + (+7)$
   $= (-1) + (+7) = (+6)$
   c) $(-1) - (+8) + (+2) = (-1) + (-8) + (+2)$
   $= (-9) + (+2) = (-7)$
   d) $(+4) - (-9) - (-6) = (+4) + (+9) + (+6)$
   $= (+13) + (6) = (+19)$

EXERCISE 18

1. a) -24
    b) $+1$
    c) $(-4) \times (+5)^3 = (-4) \times (+125) = (-500)$

2. a) $(-5) \times 4 \times (-6) = (+120)$ or 120
    b) $(st)^3 = (-20) \times (-20) \times (-20) = (-8000)$
    c) $(-5)^2 - (-6)^2 = (+25) - (+36)$
        $$= (+25) + (-36) = (-11)$$
    d) $(-5) + (4)(-6) = (-5) + (-24) = (-29)$

EXERCISE 19

1. a) $4(y + 3) - 3(2y - 1) = 4y + 12 - 6y + 3 = -2y + 15$ (or $15 - 2y$)
    b) $2(3s - 4t) - 5(s + 2t) = 6s - 8t - 5s - 10t = s - 18t$
    c) $-3(2z - 1) + 7(3z - 2) = -6z + 3 + 21z - 14 = 15z - 11$
    d) $6(p + q) - (q - p) = 6p + 6q - q + p = 7p + 5q$

2. a) $3(2e + f) + 4f + 5(e - f) = 6e + 3f - 4f + 5e - 5f = 11e - 6f$
    b) $t(2t + 1) - (4t - 3) - 5 = 2t^2 + t - 4t + 3 - 5 = 2t^2 - 3t - 2$

EXERCISE 20

1. a) $(t - 5)(t - 4) = t(t - 4) - 5(t - 4)$
        $$= t^2 - 4t - 5t + 20$$
        $$= t^2 - 9t + 20$$
    b) $(2p - 1)(3p + 1) = 2p(3p + 1) - 1(3p + 1)$
        $$= 6p^2 + 2p - 3p - 1$$
        $$= 6p^2 - p - 1$$
    c) $(4s + 3t)(3s - 4t) = 4s(3s - 4t) + 3t(3s - 4t)$
        $$= 12s^2 - 16st + 9ts - 12t^2$$
        $$= 12s^2 - 7st - 12t^2$$

2. a) $(3p + 2)^2 = (3p)^2 + 2(3p)(2) + (2)^2$ using $(a + b)^2 = a^2 + 2ab + b^2$
        $$= 9p^2 + 12p + 4$$
    b) $(4y - 3)(4y + 3) = (4y)^2 - (3)^2$ using $(a - b)(a + b) = a^2 - b^2$
        $$= 16y^2 - 9$$
    c) $(s - 2)(s^2 + 2s - 3) = s(s^2 + 2s - 3) - 2(s^2 + 2s - 3)$
        $$= s^3 + 2s^2 - 3s - 2s^2 - 4s + 6$$
        $$= s^3 - 7s + 6$$

EXERCISE 21

1. a) $5(2s + 3t + 4u)$
    b) $3q(4p - 3r)$
    c) $4y(4z - 1)$

2. a) $t(t + 5)$
    b) $3y(3y - 2z)$
    c) $2pq(3p + 7q - 5)$

EXERCISE 22

1. a) $\overbrace{3y + 9z} + \overbrace{by + 3bz} = 3(y + 3z) + b(y + 3z)$
        $$= (y + 3z)(3 + b)$$

    b) $\overbrace{4p + 6r} - \overbrace{2pq - 3qr} = 2(2p + 3r) - q(2p + 3r)$
        $$= (2p + 3r)(2 - q)$$

    c) $\overbrace{3x^2 - 4x} + \overbrace{6x - 8} = x(3x - 4) + 2(3x - 4)$
        $$= (3x - 4)(x + 2)$$

    d) $\overbrace{ac - bc} - \overbrace{ad + bd} = c(a - b) - d(a - b)$
        $$= (a - b)(c - d)$$

2. a) The numbers which multiplied give $+24$ and add up to $+14$ are $+2$ and $+12$.
        $x^2 + 14x + 24 = x^2 + 2x + 12x + 24$
        $$= x(x + 2) + 12(x + 2)$$
        $$= (x + 2)(x + 12)$$
    b) The numbers which multiplied give -6 and add up to $+1$ are $+3$ and -2.
        $x^2 + x - 6 = x^2 + 3x - 2x - 6$
        $$= x(x + 3) - 2(x + 3)$$
        $$= (x + 3)(x - 2)$$
    c) The numbers which multiplied give $+15$ and add up to -8 are -3 and -5.
        $x^2 - 8x + 15 = x^2 - 3x - 5x + 15$
        $$= x(x - 3) - 5(x - 3)$$
        $$= (x - 3)(x - 5)$$

EXERCISE 22 (cont.)

3. a) The numbers which multiplied give
$(+3)(+6) = +18$ and add up to $+11$ are $+2$ and $+9$.
$3x^2 + 11x + 6 = 3x^2 + 2x + 9x + 6$
$\qquad = x(3x + 2) + 3(3x + 2)$
$\qquad = (3x + 2)(x + 3)$

b) The numbers which multiplied give
$(+5)(-2) = -10$ and add up to -9 are $+1$ and -10.
$5x^2 - 9x - 2 = 5x^2 + x - 10x - 2$
$\qquad = x(5x + 1) - 2(5x + 1)$
$\qquad = (5x + 1)(x - 2)$

c) The numbers which multiplied gives
$(+4)(+3) = +12$ and add up to -8 are -2 and -6.
$4x^2 - 8x + 3 = 4x^2 - 2x - 6x + 3$
$\qquad = 2x(2x - 1) - 3(2x - 1)$
$\qquad = (2x - 1)(2x - 3)$

4. a) $(10\ 001)^2 - (10\ 000)^2$
$= (10\ 001 - 10\ 000)(10\ 001 + 10\ 000)$
$= 20\ 001$

b) $(51)^2 - (49)^2$
$= (51 - 49)(51 + 49)$
$= 2 \times 100 = 200$

4. c) $(6\frac{1}{4})^2 - (5\frac{3}{4})^2$
$= (6\frac{1}{4} - 5\frac{3}{4})(6\frac{1}{4} + 5\frac{3}{4})$
$= (\frac{25}{4} - \frac{23}{4})(\frac{25}{4} + \frac{23}{4})$
$= (\frac{2}{4})(\frac{48}{4})$
$= \frac{1}{2} \times 12$
$= 6$

5. a) $4x^2 - 9y^2$
$= (2x)^2 - (3y)^2$
$= (2x - 3y)(2x + 3y)$

b) $36a^2 - 25b^2$
$= (6a)^2 - (5b)^2$
$= (6a - 5b)(6a + 5b)$

c) $16c^2 - 1$
$= (4c)^2 - (1)^2$
$= (4c - 1)(4c + 1)$

d) $27x^2 - 12y^2$
$= 3(9x^2 - 4y^2)$
$= 3((3x)^2 - (2y)^2)$
$= 3(3x - 2y)(3x + 2y)$

EXERCISE 23

1. a) $\frac{2p}{3q}$

b) $\frac{y\cancel{(y + 3)}}{\cancel{(y + 3)}(y + 5)} = \frac{y}{(y + 5)}$

c) $\frac{x\cancel{(x - 2)}}{\cancel{(x - 2)}(x - 5)} = \frac{x}{(x - 5)}$

2. a) $\frac{5a^2}{4}$

b) $\frac{x^2}{(x - 2)\cancel{(x + 2)}} \times \frac{\cancel{(x + 2)}(x + 1)}{2x}$
$= \frac{x(x + 1)}{2(x - 2)}$

c) $\frac{3p - 6}{p^2 - p - 6} \times \frac{p + 2}{p - 2}$
$= \frac{3\cancel{(p - 2)}}{(p - 3)\cancel{(p + 2)}} \times \frac{\cancel{(p + 2)}}{\cancel{(p - 2)}}$
$= \frac{3}{(p - 3)}$

3. a) $\frac{15a}{20} - \frac{14a}{20} = \frac{a}{20}$

b) $\frac{4x}{6} - \frac{9(x - 5)}{6}$
$= \frac{4x - 9x + 45}{6}$
$= \frac{45 - 5x}{6}$
$= \frac{5(9 - x)}{6}$

c) $\frac{2(t + 2)}{(t + 1)(t + 2)} + \frac{3(t + 1)}{(t + 1)(t + 2)}$
$= \frac{2t + 4 + 3t + 3}{(t + 1)(t + 2)}$
$= \frac{5t + 7}{(t + 1)(t + 2)}$

4. $\frac{2(x + 2)}{(x - 1)(x + 5)} - \frac{1}{(x + 5)}$
$= \frac{2(x + 2)}{(x - 1)(x + 5)} - \frac{(x - 1)}{(x - 1)(x + 5)}$
$= \frac{2x + 4 - x + 1}{(x - 1)(x + 5)}$
$= \frac{\cancel{(x + 5)}}{(x - 1)\cancel{(x + 5)}}$
$= \frac{1}{(x - 1)}$

EXERCISE 24

1. $px + pq = x + r$ expand brackets

    $px - x = r - pq$ collect terms containing x

    $x(p - 1) = r - pq$ factorise

    $x = \frac{r - pq}{(p - 1)}$ divide to find x

2. $bx + ay = ab$ multiply both sides by ab

    $ay = ab - bx$ collect terms containing y

    $y = \frac{ab - bx}{a}$ divide to find y

    or $y = \frac{b(a - x)}{a}$

3. $y(x - 2) = x + 3$ multiply both sides by x–2

    $yx - 2y = x + 3$ expand brackets

    $yx - x = 2y + 3$ collect terms containing x

    $x(y - 1) = 2y + 3$ factorise

    $x = \frac{2y + 3}{(y - 1)}$ divide to find x

4. $2s = 2ut + ft^2$ multiply both sides by 2

    $2s - 2ut = ft^2$ collect terms containing f

    $\frac{2s - 2ut}{t^2} = f$ divide to find f

    or $f = \frac{2(s - ut)}{t^2}$

5. $p + 4 = 3\sqrt{q}$ add 4 to both sides

    $(p + 4)^2 = 9q$ square both sides

    $\frac{(p + 4)^2}{9} = q$ divide to find q

    or $q = \frac{(p + 4)^2}{9}$

Check your progress 3

1. $(-2)^4 = +16$, $2(-5)^2 = +50$, $(-0.9)^3 = -0.729$

    $(-3)^2 - 4(+2)(-6) = 9 + 48 = 57$,

    $(+9) \div (-\frac{1}{3}) = (+9) \times (-\frac{3}{1}) = (-27)$

    Order is $(+9) \div (-\frac{1}{3})$, $(-0.9)^3$, $(-2)^4$, $2(-5)^2$,

    $(-3)^2 - 4(+2)(-6)$

2. a) $2(-4)^2 - 3(-4) - 1 = +32 + 12 - 1 = 43$
    b) $(-5)(-3) = +15$

3. a) $2y^3 - 6y^2 - 10y$
    b) $s - 4t - 3s + 2t = -2s - 2t = -2(s + t)$

4. a) $3(5a - 3b + 4)$
    b) $3xy(3x - 4y + 5)$

5. a) $(x + 3)(3x - 2) = x(3x - 2) + 3(3x - 2)$
    $$= 3x^2 - 2x + 9x - 6$$
    $$= 3x^2 + 7x - 6$$

    b)   The factors of (-4) which add up to (-3)
    are $+1$ and -4.
    $2t^2 - 3t - 2 = 2t^2 + t - 4t - 2$
    $$= t(2t + 1) - 2(2t + 1)$$
    $$= (2t + 1)(t - 2)$$

6. a) $\frac{2(v + 1)}{v(v + 1)} - \frac{v}{v(v + 1)} = \frac{2v + 2 - v}{v(v + 1)} = \frac{v + 2}{v(v + 1)}$

    b) $3V = \pi r^2 h + 2\pi r^3$ multiply both sides by 3

    $3V - 2\pi r^3 = \pi r^2 h$ collect terms containing h

    $\frac{3V - 2\pi r^3}{\pi r^2} = h$ divide to find h

    The required formula is $h = \frac{3V - 2\pi r^3}{\pi r^2}$.

EXERCISE 25

1. a)
$$3x + 2y = 10 \ldots \ldots \text{①}$$
$$4x - y = 6 \ldots \ldots \text{②}$$

Equal coefficients method

Multiply equation ② by 2: $\quad 8x - 2y = 12 \ldots \ldots \text{③}$

Add equation ③ to equation ①: $\quad 11x = 22$
$$x = 2$$

Substitute $x = 2$ into equation ①: $\quad 6 + 2y = 10$
$$2y = 4$$
$$y = 2$$

The solution of the simultaneous equations is $x = 2, y = 2$.

Substitution method

From equation ②: $\quad 4x - 6 = y$

Substitute in equation ①: $3x + 2(4x - 6) = 10$
$$3x + 8x - 12 = 10$$
$$11x = 22$$
$$x = 2$$

Hence, using $y = 4x - 6$, we obtain $y = 2$.

b) $p = 7 - 2q$ substituted into $3p - 2q = -3$ gives
$$3(7 - 2q) - 2q = -3$$
$$21 - 6q - 2q = -3$$
$$-8q = -24$$
$$q = (-24) \div (-8) = +3$$

Hence, using $p = 7 - 2q$, we obtain $p = 7 - 6 = 1$.

The solution of the simultaneous equations is $p = 1, q = 3$.

c) $v = 7 - 2u$ substituted into $3u - 2v = 7$ gives
$$3u - 2(7 - 2u) = 7$$
$$3u - 14 + 4u = 7$$
$$7u = 21$$
$$u = 3$$

Hence, using $v = 7 - 2u$, we obtain $v = 7 - 6 = 1$.

The solution of the simultaneous equations is $u = 3, v = 1$.

2. a) Multiply the second equation by 2: $\quad 4s = 6t + 4$

Leave the first equation as it is: $\quad 4s = 5t + 5$

Subtract: $\quad 0 = t - 1$

so $\quad t = 1$

Substitute $t = 1$ in the first equation: $\quad 4s = 5 + 5 = 10$
$$s = 10 \div 4 = 2.5$$

The solution of the simultaneous equations is $s = 2.5, t = 1$.

b) Multiply the second equation by 2: $\quad 6f - 8g = 2$

Leave the first equation as it is: $\quad 6f - 6g = 5$

Subtract: $\quad -8g - (-6g) = 2 - 5$
$$-8g + 6g = -3$$
$$-2g = -3$$
$$g = \frac{3}{2}$$

Substitute $g = \frac{3}{2}$ in the first equation: $6f - 12 = 2$
$$6f = 14$$

$$f = \frac{7}{3}$$

The solution of the simultaneous equations is $f = \frac{7}{3}, g = \frac{3}{2}$.

EXERCISE 25 (cont.)

2. c)   The equations are: $2x - 3y = 14 \quad \ldots \; ①$
                                   $3x + 2y = -5 \quad \ldots \; ②$

   Multiply ① by 2: $4x - 6y = 28 \quad \ldots \; ③$
   Multiply ② by 3: $9x + 6y = -15 \quad \ldots \; ④$

   Add ③ and ④ : $13x = 13$
                                  $x = 1$

   Substitute $x = 1$ into ① : $2 - 3y = 14$
                                  $ - 3y = 12$
                                  $y = -4$

   The solution of the simultaneous equations is $x = 1$, $y = -4$.

3. The equations are $3n + 5p = 10$ and $n + 10p = 10$.
   The second equation gives $n = 10 - 10p$, and when this is substituted into the first
   equation it gives $3(10 - 10p) + 5p = 10$.
   Hence $30 - 30p + 5p = 10$
                        $-25p = -20$
                        $p = 0.8$

   Substituting $p = 0.8$ into $n = 10 - 10p$, we obtain $n = 10 - 8 = 2$.
   The cost of a notebook is R2 and the cost of a pencil is R0.80.

4. Using $y = 12$ when $x = 2$, $12 = 2m + c$.
   Using $y = 4$ when $x = 6$, $4 = 6m + c$.
   The solution of these simultaneous equations is $m = -2$, $c = 16$.

EXERCISE 26

1. a) $x(x + 7) = 0$
           so $x = 0$ or $(x + 7) = 0$
      Solution is $x = 0$ or $x = -7$.
   b) $(y - 4)(y + 4) = 0$
           so $(y - 4) = 0$ or $(y + 4) = 0$
      Solution is $y = 4$ or $y = -4$.
   c) $(2t - 5) = 0$ or $(t + 3) = 0$
      Solution is $t = 2.5$ or $t = -3$.

2. a) $(x - 3)(x - 4) = 0$
           so $(x - 3) = 0$ or $(x - 4) = 0$
      Solution is $x = 3$ or $x = 4$.
   b) $(p - 6)(p + 1) = 0$
           so $(p - 6) = 0$ or $(p + 1) = 0$
      Solution is $p = 6$ or $p = -1$.
   c) $(n + 4)(n + 4) = 0$
           so $(n + 4) = 0$ or $(n + 4) = 0$
      Solution is $n = -4$ (repeated).

3. a) $x^2 - 13x + 36 = 0$
           so $(x - 4)(x - 9) = 0$
      Solution is $x = 4$ or $x = 9$.
   b) $2y^2 - 3y - 2 = 0$
           so $(y - 2)(2y + 1) = 0$
      Solution is $y = 2$ or $y = -\frac{1}{2}$.
   c) $t^2 + 4t - 12 = 0$
           so $(t - 2)(t + 6) = 0$
      Solution is $t = 2$ or $t = -6$.

4. If the boy's present age is n years,
           then $n^2 = 9(n - 2)$.
      hence, $n^2 - 9n + 18 = 0$
           so $(n - 3)(n - 6) = 6$
                and $n = 3$ or $n = 6$

   The present age could be 3 years
   or 6 years.

EXERCISE 27

1. a)   16 has to be added. $x^2 - 8x + 16 = (x - 4)^2$
   b)   25 has to be added. $y^2 + 10y + 25 = (y + 5)^2$
   c) $(\frac{3}{2})^2$ has to be added. $t^2 + 3t + \frac{9}{4} = (t + \frac{3}{2})^2$
   d) $(\frac{2}{3} \times \frac{1}{2})^2 = (\frac{1}{3})^2$ has to be added. $u^2 + \frac{2u}{3} + \frac{1}{9} = (u + \frac{1}{3})^2$

EXERCISE 27 (cont.)

2. a)
$$x^2 - 8x = 9$$
$$x^2 - 8x + 16 = 9 + 16$$
$$(x - 4)^2 = 25$$
$$x - 4 = 5 \text{ or } x - 4 = -5$$
$$x = 9 \text{ or } x = -1$$

b)
$$y^2 + 10y + 16 = 0$$
$$y^2 + 10y = -16$$
$$y + 10y + 25 = -16 + 25$$
$$(y + 5)^2 = 9$$
$$y + 5 = 3 \text{ or } y + 5 = -3$$
$$y = -2 \text{ or } y-8$$

c)
$$t^2 + 3t = 1$$
$$t^2 + 3t + \frac{9}{4} = 1 + \frac{9}{4}$$
$$(t + \frac{3}{2})^2 = \frac{13}{4}$$
$$t + \frac{3}{2} = \pm\sqrt{\frac{13}{2}}$$
$$t = \frac{-3}{2} \pm \frac{\sqrt{13}}{2}$$
$$t = \frac{-3 + \sqrt{13}}{2} \text{ or } t = \frac{-3 - \sqrt{13}}{2}$$
$$t = +3.303 \text{ or } t = -3.303$$
(to 3 decimal places).

> when you use your calculator, work out the numerator and don't forget to press $\boxed{=}$ before you $\div$ by 2

d)
$$3u^2 + 2u = 7$$
$$u^2 + \frac{2}{3}u = \frac{7}{3}$$
$$u^2 + \frac{2}{3}u + \frac{1}{9} = \frac{7}{3} + \frac{1}{9}$$
$$(u + \frac{1}{3})^2 = \frac{22}{9}$$
$$u + \frac{1}{3} = \frac{\pm\sqrt{22}}{3}$$
$$u = -\frac{1}{3} \frac{\pm\sqrt{22}}{3}$$
$$u = \frac{-1 + \sqrt{22}}{3} \text{ or } u = \frac{-1-\sqrt{22}}{3}$$
$$u = 1.230 \text{ or } u = -1.897$$
(to 3 decimal places).

EXERCISE 28

1. a) $a = 5, b = 9, c = 2$ and $ac = 10$

so $x = \frac{-9 \pm \sqrt{81 - 40}}{10}$

$= \frac{-9 \pm 6.403}{10}$

Solution is $x = -0.260$ or $x = -1.540$
(to 3 decimal places).

b) $y^2 - 4y - 1 = 0$
so $a = 1, b = -4, c = -1$ and $ac = -1$

$y = \frac{+4 \pm \sqrt{16 - 4(-1)}}{2}$

$= \frac{+4 \pm \sqrt{16 + 4}}{2}$

$= \frac{+4 \pm 4.472}{2}$

Solution is $y = 4.236$ or $y = -0.236$
(to 3 decimal places).

c) $a = 1, b = 1, c = -3$ and $ac = -3$

so $t = \frac{-1 \pm \sqrt{1 + 12}}{2}$

$= \frac{-1 \pm 3.606}{2}$

Solution is $t = 1.303$ or $t = -2.303$
(to 3 decimal places).

2. a) $n^2 - 5n + 3 = 0$
so $a = 1, b = -5, c = 3$ and $ac = 3$

$n = \frac{+5 \pm \sqrt{25 - 12}}{2}$

$= \frac{+5 \pm 3.606}{2}$

Solution is $n = 4.303$ or $n = 0.697$
(to 3 decimal places).

b) $a = 1, b = -6, c = -21$ and $ac = -21$

so $x = \frac{+6 \pm \sqrt{36 + 84}}{2}$

$= \frac{+6 \pm 10.954}{2}$

Solution is $x = 8.477$ or $x = -2.477$
(to 3 decimal places).

c) $a = 3, b = 1, c = -1$ and $ac = -3$

so $m = \frac{-1 \pm \sqrt{1 + 12}}{6}$

$= \frac{-1 \pm 3.606}{6}$

Solution is $m = 0.434$ or $m = -0.768$
(to 3 decimal places).

EXERCISE 28 (cont.)

3. $30(30 + L) = L^2$ so $L^2 - 30L - 900 = 0$.
    Hence, $a = 1$, $b = -30$, $c = -900$ and $ac = -900$

    $$L = \frac{+30 \pm \sqrt{900 + 3600}}{2}$$

    $$= \frac{+30 \pm \sqrt{4500}}{2}$$

    $$= \frac{+30 \pm 67.082}{2}$$

Solution of the quadratic equation is $L = 48.541$ or -18.541, but the length of the picture must be positive so the required length is 48.5 cm (to 3 significant figures).

EXERCISE 29

1. a) $3x > -6$
        so $x > -2$.
    b) $5y - 3 < 32$
        so $5y < 35$ and
        so $y < 7$
    c) $3 \geq 18 + 5t$
        so $-15 \geq 5t$ and
        so $-3 \geq t$
        Thus the solution is $t \leq -3$
        or $3 \geq 18 + 5t$
        $-5t + 3 \geq 18$
        $-5t \geq 15$ | divide by negative so change direction of sign |
        $t \leq -3$

2. $-3 \leq 2x + 3$ leads to $-6 \leq 2x$
    and so $-3 \leq x$.
    $2x + 3 < 3$ leads to $2x < 0$
    and so $x < 0$.
    Solution is $-3 \leq x < 0$.

    ●- - - - - - - - - - - ○
    ←|——+——+——+——+——+——|→
    -4 -3 -2 -1 0 1

3. $-2 \leq n < 2.5$ but n is a positive integer
    so $n = 1$ or 2.

4. The possible values of x are 1, 2, 4, 5.

Check your progress 4

1. Adding the equations gives $7x = 21$ and so $x = 3$.
    Substituting $x = 3$ in either equation gives $y = -2$.

2. a) When $x = 0$, $P = 15$ gives $b = 15$ so the formula is
        $P = ax + 15$.
        When $x = 60$, $P = 45$ gives $45 = 60a + 15$ and so
        $30 = 60a$.
        The value of a is 0.5 and the value of b is 15.
    b) The formula is $P = 0.5x + 15$.
        When $x = 100$, $P = 50 + 15 = 65$.
        The pressure at a depth of 100 m is 65.

3. a) $\boxed{2\,|\,9} = 10 \times 2 + 9$
    b) (i) $\boxed{q\,|\,p} = 10q + p$
        (ii) $\boxed{p\,|\,q} - \boxed{q\,|\,p}$
             $= (10p + q) - (10q + p)$
             $= 10p + q - 10q - p$
             $= 9p - 9q$
    c) (i) $9p - 9q = 18$ which can be simplified
            to $p - q = 2$.
        (ii) The simultaneous equations $p - q = 2$ and
             $p + q = 14$ give $p = 8$ and $q = 6$.
        (iii) The number is $10p + q = 10(8) + 6 = 86$.

4. $(2y + 5) = \pm 7$ so $2y = 2$ or -12.
    Hence, the solution is $y = 1$ or $y = -6$.

5. a) $y = 2$ when $x = 1$ so $2 = a + b$
        $y = -5$ when $x = 2$ so $-5 = \frac{a}{2} + 2b$
        and so $-10 = a + 4b$.
        The simultaneous equations $a + b = 2$ and
        $a + 4b = -10$ give $a = 6$ and $b = -4$.
    b) The formula is $y = \frac{6}{x} - 4x$. When $y = 16$,
        $$16 = \frac{6}{x} - 4x$$
        Multiply both sides by x: $16x = 6 - 4x^2$
        $$4x^2 + 16x - 6 = 0$$
        Divide both sides by 2: $2x^2 + 8x - 3 = 0$
    c) $a = 2$, $b = 8$, $c = -3$ and $ac = -6$
        The solution of the equation is
        $$x = \frac{-b \pm \sqrt{b^2 - 4ac}}{2a}$$
        so $x = \frac{-8 \pm \sqrt{64 + 24}}{4}$
        $$= \frac{-8 \pm 9.381}{4}$$
        Solution is $x = 0.35$ or $x = -4.35$ (to 2 decimal places).

6. $7 < 3 - 2x$ gives $2x < -4$ and so $x < -2$.
    $3 - 2x \leq 13$ gives $-10 \leq 2x$ and so $-5 \leq x$.
    The solution is $-5 \leq x < -2$.

    ●- - - - - - - - - ○
    ←|—+—+—+—+—+—+—+—+—+—+—|→
    -6 -5 -4 -3 -2 -1 0 1 2 3 4

7. a) Greatest value of $x + y = $ greatest value of $x + $
        greatest value of $y = (-3) + (2) = -1$.
    b) Greatest value of $xy = (-5)(-1) = 5$.
    c) Greatest value of $x^2 y = (-5)^2(2) = (25)(2) = 50$.

Index